The Tide is Running Out

The Tide is Running Out

What the English Church Attendance Survey reveals

Dr Peter Brierley

This survey was sponsored by:

The Centre for Black & White Christian Partnership
Campaigners
Christian Aid
Christian Book Club
Christian Healing Mission
Covenanters
Church Pastoral Aid Society
Ecclesiastical Insurance Group
English Heritage
Moorlands Bible College
Operation Mobilisation
Premier Radio
Scripture Union
Youth For Christ

*All royalties from this book will go towards
the cost of further research for the church*

Christian Research

The right of Peter Brierley to be identified
as author of this work has been asserted by him
in accordance with the Copyright, Designs
and Patents Act 1988

First British edition 2000

ISBN 1 85321 137 0

Published by
Christian Research
Vision Building,
4 Footscray Road,
Eltham,
London SE9 2TZ
Phone: 020 8294 1989
Fax: 020 8294 0014
Email: admin@christian-research.org.uk
Web: www.christian-research.org.uk

British Library Cataloguing Data
A catalogue record for this book is available
from the British Library.

Designed and produced for the publisher by
Paul Jones Associates, 98 Eden Way, Beckenham, Kent BR3 DH

Copyright © Peter Brierley 2000

Contents

Foreword

by the Archbishop of York,
the Most Rev Dr David Hope

It is attributed by Disraeli to Mark Twain that there are three kinds of lies – "lies, damned lies and statistics", which does not bode well for the art of the statistician.

Peter Brierley has done it again in publishing the results of this latest English Church Attendance Survey. And the point is that it is by way of helpful information to the churches to assist them in discerning the trends and thereby plan for the future. Peter Brierley does not leave us with a mass of figures – though he certainly produces masses of figures for us. The attraction of this book is that its author seeks both to inform and to interpret.

No doubt the media will seize on the fact that Sunday attendance in almost all the "institutional" churches continues to decline. However, there emerges from this publication a far more complex and therefore intriguing and interesting number of facts and trends. We need to be noting the rising number of those attending worship during the week; of those increasing numbers attending midweek church activities and significant numbers of people enlisting on enquiry courses such as Alpha. So there is some good and encouraging news here; the question to the churches is how best and most effectively are we to respond?

The real challenge of these findings, however, is the need for teaching and communicating the Christian faith and life to children and young people – a very necessary priority for any church as we prepare to enter the third Christian millennium.

Peter Brierley and Christian Research deserve our thanks and appreciation both for the challenge which their statistics present us and as well for some of the more confident pointers to the future.

+David Ebor:

Executive Summary

This book contains the results of the 1998 English Church Attendance Survey, a two-page questionnaire sent to every church in England and answered by 33% of them. The results give a picture of church life in the 1990s. The top 12 key findings are as follows:

- The steep decline in numbers attending church on Sunday in the 1980s has continued at about the same rate in the 1990s. [Chapter 2]

- The actual decline in the 1990s has been made much worse by the large numbers of churchgoers (about a third) now attending less frequently than they used to.   [Chapter 3]

- Whereas 12% of the English population went to church weekly each Sunday in 1979, and 10% in 1989, this has dropped to 7.5% in 1998.
[Chapter 2]

- A further 2.7% attend once or twice a month, and 6.0% more less frequently.   [Chapter 3]

- Many attend worship services during the week instead of Sunday, equivalent to a further 0.9% of the population, half in adult services and half at special youth events. A further 2.4% of the population go to mid-week church activities but do not attend church on Sunday.   [Chapter 7]

• Many others are involved in church like activities but not at church, such as the 1.9% of the population who watch *Songs of Praise* but who do not go to church, or the 0.4% of the population at an Alpha course.   [Chapters 4 and 7]

• There is however a very serious decline in the number of children (under 15 years of age) attending church. We are currently losing 1,000 a week (net).   [Chapter 4]

• The number of older people, 65 or over, attending church on Sunday, however, is increasing, with 32,000 more in 1998 than in 1989.   [Chapter 4]

• One person in 8 going to church is non-white, double the percentage in the general population.   [Chapter 5]

• In the late 1990s far fewer new churches were being started than in the early 1990s.   [Chapter 8]

• Evangelicals have declined less than non-evangelicals; the Mainstream have grown while Broad and Charismatic Evangelicals have declined.   [Chapter 6]

• The Charismatics however have the greatest expectancy of significant growth by 2010, but they account for only 14% of all English churchgoers.   [Chapter 9]

The tide is running out. We need leaders and lay people of energy and vision who can implement strategic cultural change in the church for a vibrant 21st century impact.

1: Here we go again!

Large scale exercises are important from time to time. Near where my mother lives in Shooters Hill, south London, there is a beautiful view looking over the whole of north west Kent. On a clear day you can see the nearby towns of Welling and Gravesend quite clearly, but also many miles beyond them. The nearby golf course is put into the perspective of a panorama of rolling fields and hazy settlements as far as the eye can see. The view gives the framework for the detail. If I want to watch people playing golf or focus on the pollution caused by the industry near the River Thames, I can do so conscious of the wider picture to which it belongs. It is exactly the same for big surveys. They give the overview, paint the broad picture, into which the ups and downs of individual aspects fit.

So why another survey?

The 1998 English Church Attendance Survey, ECAS for short, was carried out precisely for that purpose. We needed to have a broad picture of the church to get a feel of the context into which the work and witness of the many churches of our land may be put. Not everything is uniform, and by focussing on specific areas of interest we can learn better the story of what God is doing today.

"Why do we want another big national survey?" someone said, "Don't we know the answers already?" It might be easy to assume so. Church attendance was 12% of the population in 1979, and the 1989

English Church Census gave it as 10%, so it isn't necessary to be a mathematician to work out it could be 8% by 1999. As we shall see, the 8% figure, predictable as it may seem, is in fact optimistic.

Trends. We can see how the figures emerging from the present study compare with the previous ones, and see what is growing and what isn't, and seek to learn from that process. National surveys are not just giant exercises to test if our computers are working properly or satisfy researchers who like to do things on a big scale. Their whole purpose is to glean useful information which we can apply to our work. When I lecture on the interpretation of information I always say that there are two elements to look for in statistics – the overall strength (what is the number?) and how is it moving (where is it going?). The second is as important as the first. Trend information gives us this second vital element of understanding what is happening in the world, and in English church life in particular. So building on the results of the English Church Census of 1989 becomes crucial.

*"...what makes me think it's this weekend the
Vicar's completing his 'church attendance' survey form?..."*

Credit: Taffy Davies, Church of England Newspaper, 11th September 1998

Future. Past trends give a basis for projecting into the future. This may not be as easy as it sounds, and there are many ways to forecast. However it is attempted, it is always important to see what the future may be like if existing trends continue unchanged. Experience suggests that existing trends are very unlikely to continue unchanged but at least projecting ahead on that basis gives us information to steer by. A ship needs the lighthouse beam way ahead so that if it appears to be heading for danger it can change course. It was because information being received was disregarded it was too late to save the *Titanic* when eventually the look out cried, "Ice ahead!" Looking ahead is vital, and forecasting is one way of attempting that.

Change. Much has changed during the 1990s and not only the government! A fresh national survey at the end of the 1990s allows us to see what impact, if any, such changes have had on the church, and to evaluate their significance. Such reflection is vital in order to assess whether certain undertakings should be repeated, and, if so, whether in an identical or modified form.

Strategy. Assessing change, understanding trends, evaluating the future, looking at the national picture, all build up into the importance of taking strategic action. A spokesperson for the new Archbishops' Council, meeting for the first time in January 1999, said that part of that Council's work was to think strategically about the future. That's tremendous! The church badly needs concerned strategic initiatives to take it strongly into the next millennium with confidence and perception.

So this ECAS study was undertaken for all these reasons. It might still be asked if such surveys need to be taken every few years. The answer is YES, because of the many changes that occur in each decade both in the Church and in the national and international scene which affect the church.

What have been the main changes?

The ordination of women. After a long struggle, the General Synod of the Church of England finally agreed to the ordination of women in November 1992, with the first ordinations actually taking place in May 1994, after the enabling legislation was in place. Not everyone agreed with this vote, and about 300 priests left the Church of England. Many joined the Roman Catholic Church, some the Greek or Russian Orthodox Church, and a few set up alternative Anglican congregations (58 at the end of 1997[1]).

Church planting. There has been a considerable emphasis on church planting by all the major denominations. The Archbishop of Canterbury, the Most Rev George Carey, speaking at a Church Growth Conference in May 1991, shortly after his appointment, gave his approval to the Anglican church participating in such experiments. Challenge 2000 organised two conferences, in 1992 and 1995, to promote the importance of such activity. The Elim Pentecostal Church has had a special focus on church planting especially in the North West. Kensington Temple, in central London, has started many new churches in and around London. The various New Church streams see church planting as a crucial method of evangelism. The Baptist and Methodist churches have approved and urged the formation of such new congregations.

Major campaigns. The Pentecostal Jesus In Me was a major campaign in 1994 advertised very widely on hoardings. The same year Reinhard Bonnke of Germany aimed to post a gospel to every household in Britain in time for Easter.

Alpha initiative. Rev Nicky Gumbel, then curate at Holy Trinity, Brompton, London, held the first Alpha course in the church in 1992. Within 7 years its popularity had swept the country, and indeed many countries around the world. There was a national campaign to invite the entire population to an Alpha course in September 1998 with over 6,300 participating churches, which was repeated in 1999.

Rise in cohabitation. The 1990s have seen a massive swing away from marriage into cohabitation first. This affects mostly those in their twenties, among whom in 1993 14% of men aged 16 to 24 and 12% of women were cohabiting. What percentage of couples marrying in church had cohabited first (based on the number who gave same address when registering)? In an article in the government journal *Population Trends*[2], the figure of 41% was given for England and Wales, but it was suggested this could be an under estimate of up to 20%. This would mean that at least three couples in five marrying in church cohabit first. Those who do cohabit however often realise that most churches' teaching is against this practice, and therefore rarely, if ever, attend church (though this may not be their sole reason for non-attendance at church).

Sunday Shopping. Legislation passed in 1994 allowed shops to open for 6 hours on a Sunday. Has this impacted church attendance by detracting from traditional Sunday activity? It obviously affects those who work in shops as well as accompanying service industries and makes morning church attendance much more difficult for them if not impossible. Not that churchgoers shop on Sunday particularly – one survey showed only 8% did as against 60% of the rest of the population – but the law has engendered a culture change in English society which has affected churchgoers along with the rest. Whether this will change again if key shops do not open on Sunday remains to be seen; Boots in Gloucester and Marks & Spencer in Derby for example are closing because of lack of Sunday trade[3].

Competition. Sunday shopping is not the only competitor. Many schools and sports clubs have fixtures on a Sunday morning, thereby making it more difficult for some children to get to Sunday School. In addition, many churches are finding it harder to get Sunday

School teachers willing and able to teach each week, moving to a rota system instead. Children find it harder to relate to different teachers on successive weeks, especially if they are irregular themselves. In addition, alternative activities, especially visiting friends and relatives, or, children's instrumental classes, or with the increasing divorce rate including Christian couples, the need to make Sunday "Daddy's day" all create alternative priorities, and churchgoing suffers as a consequence.

Revival. There seems to have been much more talk of revival in the 1990s than there was in the 1980s. Gerald Coates, Pioneer leader, has regularly spoken of the revival in Christianity amongst the nation's gypsies, and the prison population. Meetings in Emmanuel Church, Marsham Street, central London, opposite the offices of the Department of Environment regularly pray for revival and have inspired many thousands to find Christ. A number of books have been published on revival, which is seen as the outworking of many prophecies. Revival can be defined in different ways, but on the basis of more new people joining the church, this was probably more true in England in the 1980s than in the 1990s. An estimate published in 1996 suggested that a revival might add 5% to the churchgoing population in 4 years[4].

Post-modernity. Although the seeds were sown much earlier, and the ideas were being expressed by name in the latter 1980s, the 1990s have seen the flowering of what has come to be called "Post-modernity". Many books have been written on its meaning, but it has been helpfully summed up[5] as having five key elements:

- Spirituality without Christianity
- Environment without a Creator
- Words without meaning
- Individuality without belonging
- The present without a future.

All these affect Christianity in one way or another. For example, the words "Christian" and "church" have changed meaning, while increasing individuality encourages more people to consider church-going as a choice rather than a lifestyle.

Post-evangelicals. The evangelicals were the group growing most rapidly in the 1989 English Church Census. The New Churches and Pentecostals, the two fastest growing denominations[6], are evangelical. The present leader of the Church of England, Archbishop George Carey is known to be an evangelical. Several politicians are, as are Cliff Richard and others in the entertainment world. The list could easily be extended. Then in 1992 a book by an ex-New Church leader, Dave Tomlinson, entitled *The Post-Evangelicals*, argued that evangelicals need to keep abreast of modern critical Biblical scholarship, and get to grips with the world as it is. This book has had a wide influence, perhaps especially in the Church of England, of which Dave Tomlinson is now a minister. A few churches in the ECAS study defined themselves as "post-evangelical".

Changing church attendance. Pressure became obvious in the 1990s that some church people were attending church less than previously, and this not because of illness or disbelief. The Diocese of Ripon conducted experiments to measure attendance and found it to be true. One minister told me, "The people who used to come twice a Sunday now come twice a month." The importance of this change is fundamental, and was one of the key reasons for the present study. This is explored in depth later.

Time pressure. Pressure is hard to measure. In recent decades people always seem to be busy. Perhaps because of the recession, when jobs became fewer, those in employment worked longer hours to try to ensure they stayed in employment thus adding pressure to their lives. More people today seem to be very busy developing and maintaining a prosperous, comfortable lifestyle, and this naturally includes churchgoers. If you are under pressure, is your priority (as a committed Christian) always to go to church on a Sunday? More seem to be saying NO!

Information Technology (IT). The 1990s have seen a dizzying display of ever dazzling technology with chips everywhere! The computer has expanded its use beyond recognition in the last 9 years, and is likely to continue changing at an astronomical speed. Patrick Dixon's book *Futurewise*[7] spells the F of FUTURE as meaning "Fast" and he applies this to IT. The World Wide Web has grown dramatically, and communications between people through it are altered for ever. That includes the church as well, even if some people feel the church is slower than other organisations in learning to take advantage of it. Even if this was true in the past, that is rapidly becoming less so now. A book published in 1999[8] listed a thousand Christian Websites, for example.

All this adds up to massive change in the last decade, and it became important to assess the cumulative impact of it all on church people in respect of church attendance. And the 1990s has been the Decade of Evangelism for many churches, acting as a broad catalyst for change of emphasis or priority.

So how was the Survey carried out?

The English Church Census of 1989 by MARC Europe, a charity supported by World Vision, had 3 sponsors. In the early 1990s World Vision decided not to support anything for which they were not directly raising money, and closed MARC Europe down. However the Board and present Director decided that the work it was doing should be kept going. The name was changed to the more appropriate Christian Research, and it remains a charity and a company limited by guarantee. However there is no organisation like World Vision behind it now.

As a consequence it was necessary to seek sponsors for the English

Church Attendance Survey, and altogether 14 organisations were willing to help. They are listed on the title page. Some of these are denominational bodies; most are interdenominational; some are secular organisations working with churches or church people.

Administration

The survey form was drawn up by Christian Research and piloted. We are very grateful to those churches included in that sample for completing the survey twice. A copy of the form is given in the Appendix. It was mailed to all the churches in England, using the address list compiled by MARC Europe for the English Church Census and updated since by Christian Research (though with fewer resources not always so completely). Some churches were found to have closed with 37,717 the number of churches believed to be currently open.

The survey covered all Christian denominations, including all Free, Protestant, Anglican, Roman Catholic and Orthodox Churches, that is, all those accepting the Trinitarian formula of belief in God the Father, God the Son and God the Holy Spirit in one Essence. This excludes the Jehovah's Witnesses, Mormons, Christian Scientists, Christadelphians, Jews, Muslims, Hindus and members of other non-Trinitarian or non-Christian groups. Collectively the religious people thus excluded represented 7% of the UK population in 1995[9].

"Church" was defined for the purpose of this study as a body of people meeting on a Sunday in the same premises primarily for public worship at regular intervals. It included normal church buildings, groups meeting for worship in school chapels and armed forces chaplaincies, but not those in hospital or prison. Churches who meet on Saturdays (like the Seventh Day Adventists, or Catholics taking Vestigial Mass) were also included. Churches whose services are held fortnightly or monthly were counted in, but not those used less frequently. Congregations who do not own a building but hire a local school or civic hall for their meetings were included.

Unlike the English Church Census, prior publicity was minimal. As far as most ministers were concerned, the first they knew about it was when the two colour form arrived asking them to complete it within a month. The prime reason for less publicity was lack of financial resources. This survey was undertaken for a fifth of the price of the Census, although the Census had to spend substantial sums constructing the mailing list for all the churches. MARC Europe was well known at the time of the English Church Census, and although the change to Christian Research took place in 1993 it has a lower profile, even though it publishes the *UK Christian Handbook*!

Another difference was in the objections expressed. Intellectual arguments were put up against the English Church Census study (such as "David was punished for conducting his census", or "the emphasis we have is on quality not quantity", or "such data collection is unnecessary"). Only a handful of people objected to the English Church Attendance Survey on such grounds. Many more protested at the lack of notice, or that they simply did not have time to organise it.

This last factor was expressed again and again, sometimes with explanations like "This is the tenth survey we have been asked to complete this year, and we simply can't do any more." One Anglican vicar wrote, "This year we have already completed surveys on prayer, Bible study, non-white Anglicans, youth work, the Greater Churches Group, as well as annual surveys for the Diocese and English Heritage ... I'm afraid I shall have to refuse!" The sheer volume of such studies militates against extra ones.

In secular surveys, the reasons for non-response are also occasionally surveyed! One in 1999 gave the following reasons for not replying: "I am too busy at the moment" (81%), "We receive too many questionnaires" (78%), "The questionnaire is too long" (71%), "There is no benefit for my company" (66%), and "it is an inconvenient time of the year" (59%)[10]. That the questionnaire was too long was never said about the ECAS form, and the last two reasons rarely. The huge majority of ministers giving a reason for not taking part would have agreed with one or both of the first two categories.

A covering letter sent with the form stressed the confidentiality of the numerical information given. The analyses given here and elsewhere do not allow the recognition of the results of any participating church. The form also asked for names and addresses of youth and other church leaders; these likewise are protected under the terms of the Data Protection Act. Some respondents were however hesitant to supply such names and addresses, and therefore declined also to give answers to the data questions. Perhaps phone salesmen put many off giving names for more worthy causes!

A survey not a census

This study was deliberately not called a Census. It did not ask for an accurate count of people attending church on a particular Sunday, as had the 1989 Census. It simply asked for the "average number on a typical Sunday in September 1998". Precision was not required partly because of the firm base of the 1989 study, but much more because the actual meaning of "attendance" was fluctuating, and the survey was designed to measure that. A Census requires strict accuracy; this survey was looking at broader issues.

Response

The response was statistically very good, but nevertheless was significantly lower than the 1989 Census. Two of the reasons have been given above: the lack of prior publicity, and the time pressure upon so many ministers. In addition, the Church of England informed Dioceses that this survey was not their preferred way to collect such data, and a number of Anglican churches did not reply as a consequence.

Other denominations however warmly welcomed it. Many

Divisional Commanders in the Salvation Army commended it to their corps, for example, and several Catholic bishops wrote supporting it. Other senior leaders also indicated the importance they attached to this kind of study and urged their colleagues to complete the form. The survey was mailed at the beginning of September 1998, and reminders were posted 6 or 8 weeks later. All those who replied up to the third week of February 1999 were included. Some churches, especially the Black ones, were phoned for replies in November and December. The Methodists and Roman Catholics make their normal denominational returns in October so many of these delayed sending their form back and completed the two simultaneously.

Responses came from a total of 12,446 churches, almost exactly one third, 33%, of all the 37,717 churches in England. The numbers of forms returned is more than sufficient to give answers to the basic questions the English Church Attendance Survey was seeking, though not as accurately as in the 1989 Census. The response rates by denomination were:

Churches in smaller denominations	61%
Roman Catholic Churches	50%
Baptist Churches	44%
Independent Churches	39%
New Churches	39%
United Reformed Church	38%
Pentecostal Churches	31%
Methodist Churches	29%
Anglican Churches	25%
Orthodox Churches	15%

Estimates have been made for those who did not respond, partly on the basis that their figures would on average be similar to those who did respond, but also by comparing the resulting totals to see if the trend in their figures was reasonable compared with the previous study or with published denominational or other figures.

Accuracy

The 1989 English Church Census was built on a similar but more limited Census in 1979. After completing the 1989 Census it was realised that a number of newly started churches had been omitted, since in the 1980s there were many such churches and it was impossible to keep totally up-to-date records. Inadvertently also some Anglican children were counted both as those attending Sunday School, and as adults attending Sunday services. Both these corrections have been incorporated into 1989 figures quoted for comparison.

The statistical accuracy of any survey is dependent on three things: the actual level of accuracy desired (usually taken on what is technically called a 95% confidence interval, though other percentages are perfectly possible); the percentage value emerging from the results (percentages closer to 50% are slightly less accurately measured than smaller percentages), and the number on which the percentage is based. Of these the last is the most important.

To illustrate these variations, take the overall 1998 finding that 7.5% of the population attend church on Sunday. Because it was based on a response of only 33% of the churches this figure is subject to a variation of ±0.5%, that is, the true figure is between 7.0% and 8.0%. Had we had the same response in 1998 as we had in 1989 (70%) the variation would have been ±0.3%, that is, between 7.2% and 7.8%[11].

In reality what is the outcome of the 1998 sample survey with the results as given by the various denominations? The 1979 and 1989 Censuses gave separate figures for adults and children, but since we are looking at total Sunday attendance these figures are combined except when age is analysed. Many denominations however give adult and child figures separately, so in the following table these too are added together, with an estimate of 20% of Roman Catholic attendance being children in 1998 (down from 24% in 1989) as the Catholic church only notes total attendance at Mass which includes older children.

Table 1: Comparison of actual figures and ECAS estimates

	C of E	RC	Methodist	URC
1995	1,081,000	1,305,500	421,967	n/a
1996	1,045,300	1,278,300	408,621	n/a
1997	n/a	1,252,900	389,289	122,468
1998	n/a	n/a	373,899	n/a
ECAS 1998	**980,600**	**1,224,000**	**373,100**	**121,700**

The closeness of these figures suggests that the overall results at least for these four major denominations are reasonable, and on that basis, it is assumed that the other figures likewise will probably be of the right order of magnitude, and that the conclusions drawn are likely to be correct.

NOTES

1. Brierley, Dr Peter, editor, *Religious Trends,* No 1, 1998/99, 1997, Christian Research, London, Table 2.18.
2. Article by John Haskey, "Spouses with identical addresses before marriage: an indicator of pre-marital cohabitation", *Population Trends,* Office for National Statistics, London, Autumn 1997, Number 89, Page 13.
3. Article in *Day One* magazine, May-August 1999, Page 3.
4. Introduction to *UK Christian Handbook,* 1996/97 edition, Christian Research, London, Page 28.
5. By my colleague Heather Wraight, Assistant Director, Christian Research.
6. The word "denomination" is used although the New Churches would not describe themselves as such.
7. Dixon, Dr Patrick, *Futurewise,* 1998, HarperCollins, London.
8. Blackmore, Rev Vernon, *God on the Net,* June 1999, HarperCollins, London.
9. Op cit (Item 1), Table 2.3.
10. Article "Examining motivations to refuse in industrial mail surveys" by Artur Baldauf and William Moncrief in *Journal of the Market Research Society,* Volume 41, Number 3, July 1999, Page 348.
11. For those interested the actual formula behind these figures is $P = 196 \times \sqrt{\{p(1 - p)\} \div N}$, where p is the percentage in question, and N is the number on which it is based. When $p = 7.5\%$, or 0.075, then $(1 - p)$ is 0.925. $N = 12,446$. Thus we have $P = 196 \times \sqrt{(0.075 \times 0.925 \div 12446)} = 0.46$.

2: *Bleeding to death*

Archbishop George Carey used these dramatic words when he preached in the Anglican Cathedral of St Mary and All Saints in Harare, Zimbabwe, at the end of the World Council of Churches' Assembly in December 1998. "The crisis that I see world Christianity facing in our generation can be simply put," he said, using "crisis" as meaning a "moment of decision which may either end in opportunity or in judgement". "If our response to this crisis," he continued, "does not lead us to Christ it will surely end in decline for our churches today. ... Our mission is under attack. ... In some sections of our Western Church we are bleeding to death."[1]

Perhaps he had in mind his native country of England. The words are an apt description of where we might be going if one looks at them from a purely statistical point of view. In 1979 5.4 million people in England attended church on an average Sunday. Ten years later in 1989 that number had become 4.7 million. Nine years later in 1998 that number had become 3.7 million. A 0.7 million drop in 10 years has been followed by a 1.0 million drop in 9 years, a 13% decline over 10 years and a 22% decline over 9 years.

This has been at a time when the population has been increasing, from 46 million in 1979 to nearly 50 million by 1998. This means that Sunday church attendance, in percentage terms, has become:

- 11.7% attending church on an average Sunday in 1979
- 9.9%   in 1989, and
- 7.5%   in 1998.

A possible doomsday scenario

It would be very easy to read a doomsday scenario into such figures. They are alarming not just because they are declining, but because the rate of decline is increasing. In the first 10 year period they dropped 1.8% (11.7 less 9.9), and in the second 9 year period 2.4%, that is, 0.6% more. Suppose this rate of change continues, then in a further 9 year period (by 2007) the drop could be a further 3.0% (that is, 2.4% + 0.6%), and in the following 9 years (by 2016), 3.6% (that is, 3.0% + 0.6%). That would take the percentage going to church in 2016 down to 0.9%! Just one generation, and we would indeed have bled to death.

You can imagine newspapers creating a graph like Figure 1 below and accompanying it with headlines such as:

"CAREY VINDICATED: CHURCH BLEEDS TO DEATH"
"AFTER 2 MILLENNIA, SATAN BEATS CHRIST IN ENGLAND"
"EXIT CHURCH IN 'CHRISTIAN' ENGLAND".

Figure 1: Worst-case scenario: percentage of population attending church on Sunday

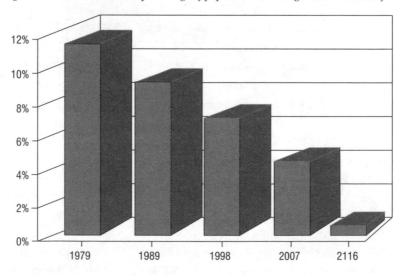

In the next 15 to 20 years the churches face an enormous challenge, with people remaining Christian but no longer attending church, or not attending as much as they used to. Nor is the challenge unique to England or the UK. One survey of Protestant attendance in America found a 9% drop in the one year 1997 to 1998[2]. David Kinnaman of the Barna Research Group in California said, "Spirituality in the United States is a mile wide and an inch deep"[3].

The challenge is as large as the one they faced in the nineteenth century, when the impact of the industrial revolution saw a massive migration from the countryside to towns and cities. Hundreds of new parishes were created, and thousands of churches of all denominations erected to provide for the spiritual needs of these people.

Is it really so bad?

If the industrial revolution did not lead to the death of the church, why should the present decline do so? Present trends rarely continue into the future exactly the same as in the immediate past. They can get worse! They can also not be as bad, and this is likely for churchgoing in the next 20 years. Decline will almost certainly continue, but not as fast as the rates I have just suggested. It is also statistically quite wrong to assume that the rate of decline will continue to increase at 0.6% per 9 years on the basis of effectively one measurement!

The huge decline, however, does not mean that Christianity is "bleeding to death" in England. People are not converting to atheism in large numbers. Rather, as David Edwards, the former Provost of Southwark Cathedral, has put it:

> Because the decline of the Churches has been so substantial ... it seems likely that for most of the English what survives of Christianity will continue to be more or less *churchless* unless the Churches become radically different.[4] [My italics]

Sunday attendance figures are important, they can be used as a trend indicator, and as an overall assessment of where Christianity is at this moment in time. However, while they are a key indicator, they are not the only one.

Another key indicator, which we look at in the next chapter, is that Sunday attendance itself is changing, with more people in total attending church than the average on one Sunday indicates. Then there are the people who come to church during the week instead of Sunday, which we also look at later. And especially for some elderly people, there are substitutes for Sunday attendance, such as *Songs of Praise*. The issue may therefore immediately be seen as being much more complicated than the "simple" Sunday attendance figures suggest.

Another complexity is that some churches are doing very well. Two London churches particularly were in the news in 1999. The Kingsway International Christian Centre (KICC) in Hackney (led by Rev Matthew Ashimolowo from Nigeria) started with a 1992 congregation of 200, but had over 6,000 every Sunday in 1999. Holy Trinity, Brompton, a charismatic evangelical church began its first Alpha course (a series of weekly meetings over a meal which include teaching on a specified element of the Christian faith) also in 1992, and has seen the number of courses grow to over 20,000 annually worldwide seven years later.

These are not the only large churches. Kensington Temple, the Pentecostal "mecca" in the London Borough of Hammersmith draws 10,000 regularly throughout its network of 130 churches. All Souls, Langham Place, Church of England, in the West End of London, has attendances of 2,000 some Sundays. There are many other large Anglican churches, with attendances between 600 and 1,000 every Sunday, such as Christ Church, Bristol, or St Mary's, Reigate, or Christ Church, Fulwood, Sheffield.

There are large Baptist churches, of similar size, such as at Altrincham near Manchester, Gold Hill at Gerrards Cross, Stopsley Baptist in Luton, or Bracknell Family Centre. There are also large Independent churches such as Above Bar Church, Southampton, or Cornerstone in Nottingham. A few Methodist, and several New Churches have congregations in excess of 500 each Sunday. Many Roman Catholic churches draw in excess of 1,000 people to Mass every Sunday, and in Liverpool the largest see over 4,000 each week. It is simply not true to say that no-one is going to church – they are!

Institutional church v non-institutional

We need to break down the total average Sunday attendance into various constituent parts. The most important of these is denomination, and we look at these initially in two broad groupings.

"Institutional" churches are defined as those denominations in which are the State Church, in at least one country in the world. There are four of these – Roman Catholic, Church of England, Orthodox and Presbyterian (the other institutional church, the Lutherans, are so small in England that they are covered in other smaller denominations, a composite group included in the non-institutional category). As the Presbyterian Church of England helped to form the United Reformed Church (URC) in 1972, the URC is taken as the equivalent for this purpose in England. "Non-institutional" churches are the other churches, broken into six groups.

Table 2 shows the total numbers, adults and children, attending church on Sunday for the three years 1979, 1989 and 1998, the first two being taken from the respective English Church Censuses, broken down between institutional and non-institutional churches. The percentage between the columns shows the change between the respective years; the two time periods are not quite equal, the first is for 10 years, the second nine.

Figure 2: Total Sunday church attendance 1979 to 1998

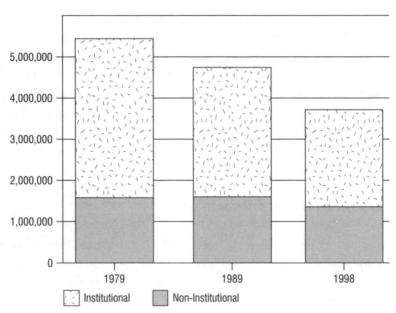

Table 2 shows that about two-thirds of English church attendance is seen in the institutional churches. It was 71% of attendance in 1979 and 63% in 1998.

Table 2: Total Sunday church attendance, 1979-1998

	1979	change	1989	change	1998
Institutional churches	3,862,000	−19%	3,143,800	−25%	2,357,600
Non-institutional churches	1,579,000	+1%	1,599,000	−15%	1,357,100
Total All England	**5,441,000**	**−13%**	**4,742,800**	**−22%**	**3,714,700**

Table 2 also shows that the major decline in Sunday attendance has taken place in the institutional churches, although the non-institutional have seen decline in the 1990s. I have written elsewhere[5] on the institutionalism that we face in Europe, where, overall, 97% of church membership is institutional. Part of the reason·is that Europe has been the seedbed of empires over the last 2,000 years, and empire is really another way of spelling institutionalism.

Institutional Christianity in general has several consequences:

- A difficulty in adapting quickly to fit the culture of the day
- Local structures which are often legally based, and hence not easily changed
- Buildings are often old, and may be protected legally from change. In 1992, in 17 of the 46 counties in England more than 80% of the Church of England churches were listed buildings!
- A tendency for their leaders to see themselves as the "guardians" of Christianity, and, as a consequence, there is less willingness to introduce radical change quickly
- The leadership is often broader theologically than non-institutional churches and have a wider range of people to be considered before change can take place
- A hierarchical bureaucracy which can inhibit radical decisions.

All of these are true for England.

Institutional church attendance

Table 3 breaks down the institutional figures in Table 2 by the four constituent denominations. The Church of England and the Roman Catholic church together represent 95% of the total in 1979 and 94% in 1998.

Table 3: Institutional churches Sunday attendance, 1979-1998

Denomination	1979	change	1989	change	1998
Roman Catholic	1,991,000	−14%	1,715,900	−28%	1,230,100
Church of England	1,671,000	−24%	1,266,300	−23%	980,600
United Reformed	190,000	−21%	149,300	−18%	121,700
Orthodox	10,000	+23%	12,300	+105%	25,200
Institutional	**3,862,000**	**−19%**	**3,143,800**	**−25%**	**2,357,600**

The Roman Catholics

The **Roman Catholic** church is the largest in England in terms of numbers present on a Sunday. They have however seen a huge decline in the last 20 years, in which the drop in the 1990s has been twice as great as that in the 1980s. This large decline in the 1990s is not unique to the Catholic church in England; it has also happened in Scotland   between 1984 and 1990 Mass attendance dropped 1%, but between 1990 and 1994 it dropped 13%[6]. The drop is partly due to the less strict application of the teaching by the Catholic church that a mortal sin is not committed if a person does not attend Mass.

The main Roman Catholic Church with its 4 Dioceses in England accounts for 99% of Mass attendance in England; there are a number of overseas Catholic churches, the largest of which is the Hungarian, which account for nearly all the remaining 1%.

The Anglicans

The **Church of England** is the largest church in England in terms of number of congregations or churches – three churches in every 7 in the country are Anglican. The Church of England is 99.5% of the Anglicans in England, the others including the Free Church of England which began in 1863, and 9 other very small groupings, some of which began as a direct consequence of the vote in 1992 to ordain women priests.

The drastic decline in attendance is the fastest since 1979 for any denominational group in England, of itself accounts for two-fifths,

40%, of the entire decline in church attendance in the country. Unlike the Catholics, the decline was as great in the 1980s as it was in the 1990s. No church can sustain losing a quarter of its people every 9 or 10 years – at this rate of loss the church really will bleed to death! In 1997 the comment made by the *Church Times* when the 1995 figures of Sunday attendance first became available was "the latest statistics show that church decline has not yet 'bottomed out'"[7]. Unfortunately, this is still true.

In the last few years the Anglicans, Methodists and Baptists have restructured their central leadership. The Anglican Archbishops' Council centralises all those elements required if radical strategic action is to be taken. That may mean firm actions will be proposed, perhaps especially to recapture its youth who are dropping out fast.

The United Reformed Church

The **United Reformed Church** may be small in attendance terms in comparison to the two giants of Catholics and Anglicans, but its rate of fall is as drastic as the Catholics. The URC is about one-tenth the size of the Roman Catholic church, but unlike them they have seen about the same percentage drop in the 1980s as in the 1990s, as has the Church of England. The URC has not declined uniformly across the country; it has seen a 60% decline in the Yorkshire/Humberside Region in these 19 years and a 59% drop in East Anglia. It grew marginally in London, by 1%, from 16,400 in 1989 to 16,600 in 1998, perhaps as a result of the work in Thames North Province where the Moderator deliberately put money "into people not buildings".

The Orthodox Churches

The **Orthodox Church** is very largely the Greek Orthodox Church in England, which accounts for 93% of the total attendance. Unlike every other denomination, the Orthodox place less importance on church attendance – the numbers attending are only about a tenth of

its membership for example, and, as we shall see, about two-thirds of
their attenders only attend at Christmas and Easter. These differences help emphasise the alternative values of their spirituality, and
perhaps partly explain why they, alone of the institutional churches,
have grown since 1979, and spectacularly so in the 1990s.   This
growth in attendance has outstripped growth in the number of
priests and congregations. However, while growth is always growth,
the actual numbers are very small and in no way compensate for the
massive losses of the other institutional churches.

Figure 3 compares the rates of decline, taking 1979 as equivalent
to 100.

Figure 3: Change in Sunday attendance in institutional churches 1979-1998

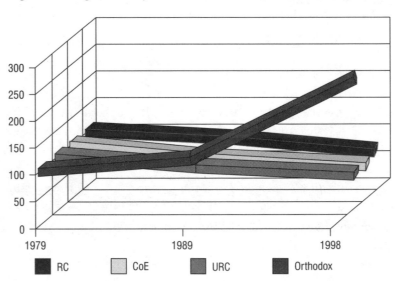

Non-institutional church attendance

Table 4 breaks down the non-institutional, or Free Churches, figures
in Table 2 by the six constituent denominations.

Table 4: Non-institutional churches Sunday attendance, 1979-1998

Denomination	1979	change	1989	change	1998
Methodist	621,000	−18%	512,300	−26%	379,700
Baptist	290,000	− 7%	270,900	+2%	277,600
New Churches	64,000	+161%	167,000	+38%	230,500
Pentecostal	228,000	+4%	236,700	− 9%	214,600
Independent	235,000	+27%	298,500	−46%	161,600
Other denominations	141,000	−19%	113,600	−18%	93,100
Non-institutional	**1,579,000**	**+1%**	**1,599,000**	**−15%**	**1,357,100**

One of these denominations has seen huge growth over the past 19 years – the New Churches. Two have largely held their own – the Baptists and Pentecostals. The other three, Methodists, Independents, and others, have sharply declined. Figure 4 shows these variations, with 1979 = 100, in the same way as Figure 3.

Figure 4: Change in Sunday attendance in non-institutional churches 1979-1998

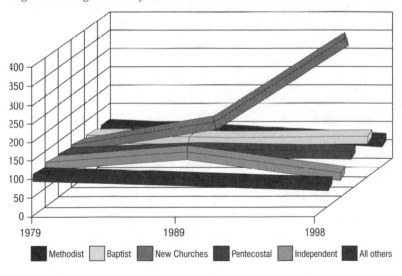

The Methodists

The **Methodists** are the second fastest declining denomination, just behind the Church of England. The Methodist Church of Great

Britain accounts for over 98% of all Methodists in England, it becoming a union of 5 separate denominations in 1932. The residual churches are largely the Independent Methodist Church and the Wesleyan Reform Union. Like the Catholics, the Methodists have declined more in the 1990s than in the 1980s.

But they do not lack energy, even if their age profile shows they have more elderly people than almost any other denomination. They have been one of the few denominations to tackle consistently the issues of homosexuality in their annual Conferences. In a totally different context, they have witnessed the growth of the work of their evangelist Rob Frost especially in his Easter People convention, which attracted over 10,000 people to Bournemouth in 1999, the large majority Methodist. According to a press report in June 1999 they are determined to stop the inexorable decline[8].

Nor is the decline unique to this country. Methodism is changing around the world. North of Wellington in New Zealand, for example, there were 40 Methodist churches in the 1950s; today there are just 3. The others have either closed or merged[9].

The Baptists

Baptists are the only denomination to be holding their own. Their decline in attendance terms was a little in the 1980s but they have grown a little in the 1990s. However the Baptist Union of Great Britain only represents 81% of Baptists in England, with the stricter Grace Baptists (6%) and Gospel Standard Strict Baptists (4%) on the one hand and the many individual independent and Old Baptists (collectively 9%) on the other making up the difference. Table 5 shows the variations each has in church attendance.

The Baptist Union figures for Sunday attendance show that just under half, 45%, of the children attached to their churches, and coming to midweek activities, actually attend on an average Sunday. Table 5 shows a growth in Sunday attendance in the 1990s.

Table 5: Baptist Sunday attendance, 1979-1998

Denomination	1979	change	1989	change	1998
Baptist Union of GB	249,400	– 9%	226,700	+2%	232,200
Grace Baptist	17,200	– 1%	17,100	– 7%	15,900
Gospel Standard	8,600	–21%	6,800	–38%	4,200
Independent Baptists	13,400	+43%	19,200	+27%	24,400
Old Baptist Union	1,400	–21%	1,100	–18%	900
Baptist	**290,000**	**–7%**	**270,900**	**+2%**	**277,600**

The Union has set up a Mission and Research Department in the last few years, and one of its first studies showed the wide range of ways in which Baptist churches were engaged with the community 44% had a parent and toddler's group, 22% a play-group, 20% ran a luncheon club, 17% transported the elderly, 12% provided clothing, 9% bereavement counselling, 8% worked with the mentally handi-capped, 8% organised recreational activities, 7% helped alcoholics, 6% worked with the unemployed, 6% ran after-school groups, 6% emergency night shelters, 6% did soup runs, 6% provided furniture, 5% ran day centres, 4% sheltered housing, etc.[10]

The three declining Baptist denominations in Table 5 have only declined in relatively small numbers numerically. The real growth is to be seen in the independent Baptist churches which have continued to grow strongly. There are many congregations in the South East, North and South, though not in Greater London or East Anglia.

New Churches

The **New Churches,** which started in the early 1970s, have seen huge growth in the two decades since then, with very strong growth in the 1980s which has continued in the 1990s but not at the same rate – attendance went up an extra 100,000 people in the 1980s but only 67,000 in the 1990s, and this from a larger base. These changes are net figures, that is, the total number of new people less those who leave.

The numbers joining and leaving New Churches are considerable.

No recent survey has been undertaken of whether those joining are people new to church or people from other denominations. A survey in the mid 1980s showed that about a third came from other churches, and that percentage may have increased in the 1990s to perhaps half. Partly this is because some attract families with children, since many New Churches put great emphasis on their children's work.

Figure 5: Proportions of key groups of New Churches by congregations, 1989 and 1998

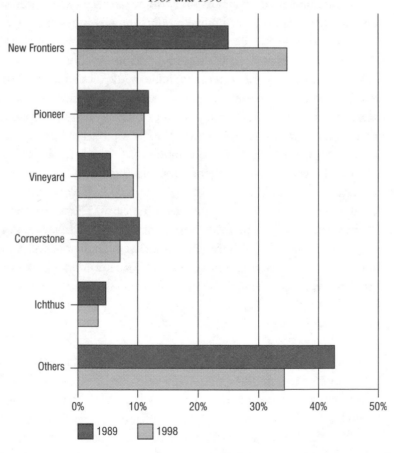

The New Churches are not a composite whole. They comprise at least 20 "streams" as the mini-denominations within the New Churches are called. The largest 5 (which would rank as full grown denominations in any other context) are New Frontiers International (NFI) led by Terry Virgo, Pioneer built through the work of Gerald Coates, the Association of Vineyard Churches started in 1987, Ichthus Christian Fellowship based in South London under Roger Forster and one of the oldest of these churches (it began in 1975), and Cornerstone in Southampton. For some of these getting precise numbers is difficult. NFI is engaged for example in dividing many of its churches into Cell Churches, where groups meet usually weekly for worship and teaching, in the context of informality and a meal.

There are a large number of individual congregations which follow New Church principles but which do not align themselves with one of the streams. The remaining New Churches divide into three broadly equal groups: New Frontiers, the other 4 large streams, and all the rest[11], as shown in Figure 5, although the Ichthus figures relate only to their London congregations, and not those affiliated to them outside Greater London.

Unfortunately in the 1989 English Church Census, the New Churches were combined with the Independent churches, so comparative attendance figures are not available by individual stream. New Churches have considerably larger attendances than membership, but the 1998 attendance figure is broken down as follows:

- 43,800 New Frontiers International
- 27,300 Ichthus Christian Fellowship
- 17,000 Covenant Ministries
- 15,400 Pioneer
- 14,600 Association of Vineyard Churches
- 9,600 Salt and Light Ministries
- 8,400 Cornerstone
- 6,700 Ground Level
- 56,200 Other New Church streams
- 31,500 Independent New churches

These attendance figures are roughly double those reported in *The Body Book*[12], the directory of charismatic churches, largely because not every New Church is listed there.

The Pentecostal Churches

The **Pentecostal** churches include the mainline, mainly white, denominations of Elim, Assemblies of God and the Apostolic Church, and also the many Afro-Caribbean churches, which are mainly black. These latter include larger denominations like the New Testament Church of God and Church of God of Prophecy. The "white" group are about 52%[13] of the total and declining, the "black" 48% and mostly growing. Table 6 gives the breakdown.

Table 6: Pentecostal Sunday attendance, 1979-1998

Denomination	1979	change	1989	change	1998
Assemblies of God	86,500	−12%	75,700	−21%	59,900
Elim Pentecostal	44,500	+13%	59,000	−25%	44,300
The Apostolic Church	5,900	+25%	7,400	−18%	6,100
New Testament Church of God	9,400*	+11%	10,400*	+41%	14,700
Church of God of Prophecy	9,100*	−13%	7,900*	−29%	5,600
All others	72,600	+5%	76,300	+10%	84,000
Pentecostal	**228,000**	**+4%**	**236,700**	**− 9%**	**214,600**

* Estimated, based on membership

Unlike many other denominations, Pentecostal attendance is always much greater than church membership. But, for the first time in their 90 year existence in the UK, Pentecostal church attendance has declined, albeit slightly. Perhaps this is because they have been planting fewer churches since 1995 (as a subsequent chapter will show) and hence their forthright evangelism has had less effect. As the New Churches have found, one of the surest ways to grow is to plant more churches.

Their decline is not uniform across the country – they have seen much growth in Greater London (aided by two large growing churches, Kensington Temple and Kingsway International and a mushrooming of smaller black churches), but also in the South East (South) and in the North West, the latter being the focus of the 1994 JIM campaign.

Table 6 shows that the main Pentecostal denominations are all in decline, and that it is only the New Testament Church of God and the miscellany of smaller black Pentecostal churches, the huge majority of which are independent of one another, which are growing.

Independent Churches

Independent churches include the Christian Brethren, both open and closed, the residual Congregational churches (the Congregational Federation and the Evangelical Fellowship of Congregational Churches (EFCC)) after the merger of the Congregational Church of England and Wales with the Presbyterian Church of England in 1972 to form the United Reformed Church, the Fellowship of Independent Evangelical Churches (FIEC) and the smaller Union of Evangelical Churches (UEC), the Churches of Christ, both Instrumental and Non-Instrumental, the various independent boarding schools with chapels, and other smaller groups[14].

The Independents grew in the 1980s but have seen a great decline in the 1990s. This decline relates not just to people but to congregations as well. Thus there are 850 fewer Independent churches in 1998 than there were in 1989. Conversely there are 650 more New Churches in 1998 than in 1989. Almost certainly part of the decline of the Independent sector has been because some of these churches have joined one of the New Church streams. Independent churches have the flexibility for doing this which other, especially the institutional, churches do not! The exact proportion of churches switching is estimated to be of the order of 500 congregations, with total attendance of at least 30,000 people.

Another reason for the decline in the Independent sector is that many of the 312 schools with chapels have stopped having boarders (the main reason), or they have stopped holding services because they were finding them so poorly attended, or holding them only occasionally rather than weekly, which would disqualify their attendance for inclusion in this survey.

A breakdown of the individual denominations within the Independent sector is given in Table 7:

Table 7: Independent churches Sunday attendance, 1979–1998

Denomination	1979	change	1989	change	1998
FIEC	63,100	+63%	102,700	–57%	43,800
Christian Brethren (Open)	64,000	+10%	70,500	–21%	49,900
Residential Schools	47,000	+7%	50,200	–67%	16,600
Congregational Federation	12,700	+20%	15,200	–28%	11,000
EFCC	9,300	+18%	11,000	–33%	7,400
Christian Brethren (Closed)	10,200	+21%	12,300	+17%	14,400
Churches of Christ	5,700	–7%	5,300	–43%	3,000
UEC	2,000	–20%	1,600	–37%	1,000
All others	21,000	+41%	29,700	–51%	14,500
Independent	**235,000**	**+27%**	**298,500**	**–46%**	**161,600**

Table 7 shows that most of the established Independent churches, which have grouped themselves into associations, fellowships, etc. have declined in attendance. Perhaps the concept of membership, which is out of favour at large in British society, is out of favour here also. Many independent churches have elderly congregations as a future Table will show and Table 7 may simply be reflecting the last stages of survival for a number of these. Certainly the picture shown here is discouraging, but if the transfers and the residential schools are excluded the overall decline reduces to –26%, which while steep, is of the order of decline for English churches generally – the overall figure was –22%. The only growing group are the Closed or Exclusive Brethren.

Other denominations

The smaller denominations are the English arm of worldwide churches, of which the largest here is the Salvation Army. The others in this category are given in Table 8.

The Religious Society of Friends and the very small groups are the two which are growing in this category. The very small groups are mostly the Holiness Churches[16] (of which the Church of the Nazarene is the largest), and the many Protestant churches for overseas nationals (Catholic ones are included in the Catholic group). Over 20 different language groups are listed in *Religious Trends*[17], of which the largest are, in order, the Chinese, Korean and the Swiss. There are also an increasing number of small groups of churches which are included here, numbering just a handful of congregations, which are neither charismatic, New Church-like, nor black (these are included elsewhere).

Table 8: Smaller denomination's Sunday attendance, 1979–1998

Denomination	1979	change	1989	change	1998
Salvation Army	107,500	−27%	78,400	−35%	51,100
Seventh-Day Adventists	14,100	+19%	16,800	−10%	15,100
Lutheran Church	8,300	−23%	6,400	−39%	4,400
Moravian Church	2,900	−14%	2,500	−36%	1,600
Religious Society of Friends	3,300	− 9%	4,100	+110%	8,600
All others	4,900	+25%	5,400	+128%	12,300
Other denominations	**141,000**	**−19%**	**113,600**	**−18%**	**93,100**

The growth of the Religious Society of Friends, very significant over the past 9 years, has been analysed[18]. 15% of the growth is internal (biological) growth (though children of Quakers are no longer automatically called members), 47% is transfer growth, mostly from the Church of England, and 38% are new people joining the Quakers because "Quakerism is an easy way to experience Christianity/religion". This last category is fluid, and not everyone stays very long. Some leave because "Quakerism is not serious enough".

Although these two groups are growing, they do not compensate for the overall decline in this category, largely because of the smaller number attending the Salvation Army. Prophecies that they will grow again have been made[19], but in the 1990s they have yet to turn the corner. For a while it was thought that their emphasis on adherents rather than soldiers (the former being less committed to the traditions of the Army than the latter) would redress the balance, but this does not appear to be the solution. They have a large number of elderly who are "promoted to glory", so the Army have to grow twice as fast as might be expected to compensate for this natural loss.

Denominational proportions

The relative strengths of the different denominations has changed slightly over the past two decades as Table 9 shows.

Table 9: Proportions each denomination is of total church attendance, 1979–1998

Denomination	1979	1989	1998	1998 as % of pop.
Roman Catholic	36.6	36.2	33.1	2.5
Anglican	30.7	26.7	26.4	2.0
Methodist	11.4	10.8	10.2	0.8
Baptist	5.3	5.7	7.5	0.6
New Churches	1.2	3.5	6.2	0.5
Pentecostal	4.2	5.0	5.8	0.4
Independent	4.3	6.3	4.3	0.3
United Reformed	3.5	3.1	3.3	0.2
Other denominations	2.6	2.4	2.5	0.2
Orthodox	0.2	0.3	0.7	0.0
Total (= 100%)	5.4mn	4.7mn	3.7mn	7.5

In 1979 it was broadly true that one churchgoer in 3 was Catholic, one Anglican and one the rest. In the next 19 years that has become less true, as Figure 6 indicates. In 1998, one churchgoer in 3 is still Catholic, but one in 4 are Anglican, and the rest the remaining 2 in every 5. The diagram also shows what the proportions might be like in 2007 if present trends continue.

Figure 6: Proportions of churchgoers by denomination 1979–1998

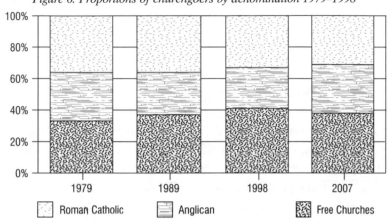

Churches of different sizes

How many large churches are there? Table 10 shows the percentages of churches of different sizes in 1998. These are not directly
comparable with similar information produced from the 1979 and
1989 studies[20] since these earlier ones not only focussed on adult
attendance only, and in the equivalent table included twice those
who came more than once on a Sunday.

Table 10: Churches of different sizes by denomination

	Free Churches %	Anlican %	Catholic %	All Churches %
1–10	3	8	0	5
11–25	17	19	1	16
26–50	17	25	2	19
51–100	28	23	7	24
101–150	12	11	7	11
151–200	9	4	9	7
201–300	7	4	19	7
301–400	3	2	16	4
401–500	1	1	12	2
500+	3	1	27	5
Total (=100%)	**17,665**	**16,281**	**3,771**	**37,717**

Table 10 shows that in England a third, 36%, have more than 100 in their Sunday congregation, a further quarter, 24%, between 51 and 100, and two churches in 5, 40%, have 50 or fewer.

There are 2,500 churches with more than 400 present, but 1,500 of these are Roman Catholic. Of the remaining 1,000, 700 are Free Church and the remaining 300 Anglican. There are 1,700 churches with congregations over 500, of which 1,000 are Roman Catholic, 540 Free Church and 160 Anglican. The larger Catholic churches are located in the urban areas, but on average 12 Free and 3 Anglican large churches might be found per county.

On the other hand, there are just under 8,000 churches with 25 or less present on a Sunday, of which under 40 are Catholic. Of the remainder, 3,500 are Free Church and 4,400 Anglican, and of the latter 1,300 have 10 or fewer in the congregation. At some stage these will become unviable.

Figure 7 illustrates Table 10, but puts the percentages as numbers of churches:

Figure 7: Number of churches with different size Sunday congregations, 1998

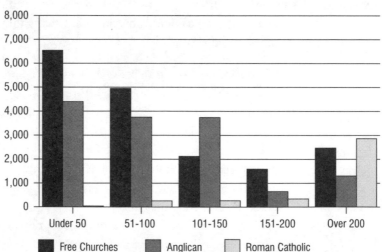

Table 10 also reveals that 45% of Roman Catholic church attenders go to just 27% of its churches. 44% of Anglican, and 41% of
Free Church churchgoers attend just 11% of their churches. Putting
this another way for the Protestant churches, half of those attending
church go to just 15% of the churches. The percentage is 18% in the
United States[21].

This comes as a consequence of "a disproportionately large number of the churchgoers born after World War II prefer(ring) the very
large churches that can respond to their demands for quality, choic-
es and specialised ministries. ... Another result is the replacement of
the neighbourhood church by the regional megachurch. A third is
the rising level of complexity that accompanies this increase in size.
A fourth is the growing demand for a high level of competence in the
professional staff."[22]

Size of church by denomination

In 1979 the average English church on an average Sunday attracted
139 people, adults and children, but only counting once those who
attended twice. However as Roman Catholics have much larger services than others, this average does not tell much. The average
Catholic church had 542 then, the rest an average of 97. This included adults and children. By 1998 these figures had become respectively 326 and 73, drops of 40% and 25%. Table 11 breaks these figures down by denomination.

Whereas in 1979 the Anglicans had the fourth smallest average
congregation, by 1998 it had the *smallest* congregation of any denomination, even smaller than the Methodists who have generally had
small congregations. The average New Church congregation is more
than double the size of the average Anglican.

The four denominations with the largest average congregations
have all engaged in church planting over the 1980s and 1990s,
although Baptists less than the others. Orthodox church "planting"
has been in reality the starting of new services in different places by

borrowing existing church buildings. As a consequence their average
congregation has decreased, part of the price of dedicating some to
pioneer elsewhere.

Table 11: Average Sunday church attendance by denomination, 1979–1998

Denomination	1979	1989	1998
New Churches	213	163	138
Baptist	131	116	115
Pentecostal	129	121	102
Orthodox	103	108	98
United Reformed	104	89	78
Other denominations	97	78	80
Independent	75	96	72
Methodist	81	76	61
Anglican	99	77	60
Average of the above	97	87	73
Roman Catholic	542	449	326

Change by churchmanship

The topic of "churchmanship" is discussed in more detail in Chapter 6,
but it is convenient to look at change by churchmanship at the same
time as change by denomination. Altogether respondents could select
up to 3 of 9 statements of the theological position of their congregation, and these have then been divided into 7 different categories, one
of which, the evangelical, is divided into 3 sub-categories.

  The same convention was followed in 1998 as adopted in 1989 of
asking the respondent to state their understanding of the churchmanship of that congregation. It is then assumed that the entire congregation would agree they were of that churchmanship. This obviously will never be true, but we assume that the excesses in one place
will even out with the deficiencies elsewhere. Only by asking every
individual within a congregation will the churchmanship of a church
be totally known. That process has been undertaken many times
with the *Congregation Attitudes and Beliefs Survey*[23], with the broad

finding that about two-thirds of a congregation usually support the churchmanship of the minister for the church.

The question was not asked in the 1979 Census, so comparisons can only be given with 1989 findings. Although 1985 figures were also available from the 1989 Census, they are not repeated here since that would the give two figures from a single source at too close a moment in time. One of the intriguing changes that has taken place has been the change in churchmanship of particular churches. This is looked at in more detail in Chapter 6, and therefore is temporarily ignored here. Table 12 gives the basic overall findings.

It must be remembered in this context that "Catholic" does not solely mean the Roman Catholic church, although many – but by no means all – Roman Catholics naturally define their churchmanship as Catholic. A number of congregations in other denominations also define themselves in this way, partly because they take the word "Catholic" in its old meaning of "universal".

Table 12: Church attendance by churchmanship, 1989 and 1998

Churchmanship	1989	change	1998
Evangelical	1,430,400	– 3%	1,391,300
Catholic	1,867,500	–48%	980,000
Liberal	479,900	–11%	425,500
Broad	434,000	–19%	352,400
Low Church	280,500	– 2%	275,400
Anglo-Catholic	178,300	0%	177,600
All others	72,200	+56%	112,500
TOTAL All England	**4,742,800**	**–22%**	**3,714,700**

It will be seen that apart from the small "others" the drop in Sunday churchgoing has been so severe that all groups have been affected. This is especially true of the Catholic grouping, showing the decline has been more than just amongst Roman Catholics; it reflects the large decline amongst the Anglicans. The Evangelicals have declined a little, mostly because of the decline amongst the Methodist, Independent and other churches, many of whom describe themselves as Broad Evangelicals.

The "others" group consists of those calling themselves Radical, those who do not name any churchmanship but instead simply repeat their denomination, and those who use a term not already on the form. In this study a number of churches opted for the last, suggesting that just as church people in the UK readily start new denominations (an average of 7 a year over the last 22 years!) so we are now also adopting new churchmanships. This at least reflects some activity as well as our individualism, and indicates a small but vociferous group which in effect is *opting out*. Why they are doing that, and what they are opting for are important, and this is part of the later discussion. Table 13 shows the percentage of the total in each category.

Table 13: Churchmanship as proportion of total church attendance, 1989-1998

Churchmanship	1989	1998	1998 as % of pop.
Evangelical	30.1	37.4	2.8
Catholic	39.4	26.4	2.0
Liberal	10.1	11.5	0.9
Broad	9.2	9.5	0.7
Low Church	5.9	7.4	0.5
Anglo-Catholic	3.8	4.8	0.4
All others	1.5	3.0	0.2
Total (= 100%)	**4.7mn**	**3.7mn**	**7.5**

The Evangelicals in 1998 were the largest theological grouping amongst churchgoers, after the great fall away by the Catholics in the 1990s. But even so they are still only just over a third of total Sunday attendance. The Catholic group is still strong and important, and is more than double the size of the nearest other group, the Liberals. The Catholic drop has allowed other smaller groups to become more important, especially the Low Church, the Liberals and the Anglo-Catholics. The last now represent one churchgoer in every 20.

Although Figure 6 contained a projection for denomination proportions for 2007, it seems unwise to produce a similar projection on the basis of the figures in Table 13. Both the Evangelical growth and the Catholic decline are too great to make it likely that these trends will continue at the same rate in the first decade of the 21st century, so Figure 8 just gives the two years 1989 and 1998.

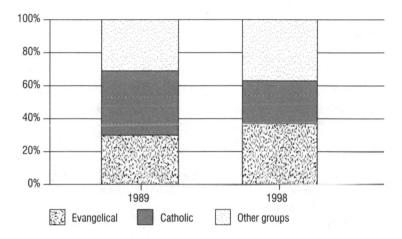

Figure 8: Proportions of churchgoers by churchmanship 1989 and 1998

Size of church by churchmanship

This is given in Table 14. Since there is such a large overlap between Roman Catholics and those with Catholic churchmanship the same problem of the size of their churches repeats, these are put separately.

Table 14: Average Sunday church attendance by churchmanship, 1989-1998

Churchmanship	1989	1998
Evangelical	105	97
Liberal	91	92
Anglo-Catholic	87	88
All others	76	83
Broad	72	71
Low Church	63	61
Average of the above	**89**	**86**
Catholic	301	156

Whilst Evangelicals have the largest congregations on average,

they are not much bigger in 1998 than those of the Liberals and
Anglo-Catholics, and the Evangelicals have seen their average congregation decline in size whereas the others have increased slightly.
This Table shows nothing like the variations seen in Table 11, showing something of the integration of the various churchmanships
across the different denominations.

The evangelicals

The evangelical category is broken down further in Table 15.

Table 15: Church attendance of Evangelicals, 1989 and 1998

Churchmanship	1989	change	1998
Mainstream	384,600	+68%	645,500
Charismatic	631,200	−16%	527,900
Broad Evangelical	414,600	−47%	217,900
All Evangelicals	**1,430,400**	**−3%**	**1,391,300**

It will be immediately obvious that a huge change has taken place
in the shape of evangelicalism in the 1990s:

- A large increase in the number of "mainstream" or mainline
  evangelicals, reflecting the increases (in order) amongst the
  Anglicans, Baptists and New Churches, the latter partly because
  of their assimilation of previously Independent churches.

- A decrease in the number of charismatics. This is partly due
  to the fact that about a quarter of the Pentecostal churches
  now do not describe themselves as "charismatic", presumably
  because they do not wish to be associated with the "Toronto
  Blessing" which came to a number of churches in the mid-
  1990s from the Vineyard Airport Church in Toronto, Canada.
  If this switch was for the moment disallowed then the 1998
  Mainstream figure would be 591,800, an increase over 1989
  of 54%, and the Charismatic figure would be 581,600, a
  decrease of 8%.

• A large decrease in the number of broad evangelicals. This is partly due to the drop in the number of Methodist churchgoers.

These changes in evangelicalism are immense. The charismatics were the dominant party in 1989, the mainstream now are. The number of churches which have swung behind this basic change is high – a 41% increase over 9 years, or an average of 200 churches per year have become mainstream evangelical. Some ministers will know they have changed churchmanship, and why. Others, perhaps, may have been confused by the terms, or at least, in true post-modern fashion, redefined the terms making them mean what each individual wanted them to mean! On this basis, these figures may have less significance than at first seems apparent.

The size of churches is likewise affected. In 1989, the average mainstream church had an average Sunday congregation of 89; in 1998 it is 106. In 1989, the average charismatic church had a congregation of 124; in 1998 it was 110, still a little larger than the mainstream churches. In 1989, the broad evangelical's average congregation was 99; in 1998 it was down to 62.

Church attendance by region

If we are bleeding to death, we are not doing so uniformly. As in many other parts of life, the South East of England is doing better than the north and west. Table 16 gives the broad detail.

Table 16 shows where the church really is haemorrhaging. In the West Midlands and East Anglia the drop in Sunday attendance in the 1990s was three times what it was in the 1980s. In the North, Yorks/Humberside, North West, East Midlands and the South West the 1990s have seen roughly twice the decline of the previous decade. In the South East, North and South, and in Greater London, the fall in the 1990s was marginally less than in the years 1979-1989.

No region has escaped a fall. But the two South East areas, together with London, are, among the largest regions. So their rel-

ative smallness of decline mitigates the seriousness of the falls outside the South East. Three people in eight, 37%, in England live in
the South East, but two-fifths, 40%, of all going to church on Sunday
are there. The overall percentage decline between 1989 and 1998 in
Sunday attendance is 22%; take away the South East, and the average drop throughout the rest of the country is 28%.

Table 16: Sunday attendance by region, 1979-1998

Region	1979	change	1989	change	1998
North	365,300	−14%	312,500	−28%	225,100
Yorks/Humberside	512,200	−16%	429,600	−33%	286,400
North West	960,500	−17%	793,100	−30%	556,800
East Midlands	384,200	−14%	328,600	−21%	260,800
West Midlands	574,800	−10%	516,700	−30%	363,000
East Anglia	250,700	−10%	224,400	−28%	162,400
South East (North)	520,400	−14%	445,300	−13%	386,900
Greater London	696,000	− 7%	649,600	− 5%	617,900
South East (South)	615,900	−12%	544,100	−12%	479,000
South West	561,000	−11%	498,900	−25%	376,400
Total All England	**5,441,000**	**−13%**	**4,742,800**	**−22%**	**3,714,700**

This is against an average decline in the South East of 9%. In
other words, Sunday church attendance has declined in England outside the South East three times the rate at which it has fallen in the
South East. The doctoral thesis of Rev Dr Gavin Wakefield, formerly Team Vicar in Chelmsford, Essex, suggests that the decline
shown in Table 15 for the South East (North) area in the 1980s may
not have been as great as indicated[24]. Those whose work at church
headquarters in London cause them to live in the South East may
not realise the seriousness of church life in other parts of England.

Why is the South East "protected"? There are a number of factors
to its advantage:

• The South East, especially Greater London, boasts a number of
  very large churches. Quite a few of those mentioned earlier are

based in London. And these churches by and large have seen considerable growth in the 1990s, which compensates for a lot of declining ones.

• There has been a steady migration of people, especially from the northern areas, towards the South East in the 1990s. In the 7 years 1991-1998, 19,000 moved out of the North East, especially Tyne and Wear, 29,000 out of Manchester, 43,000 have gone from Merseyside, 18,000 from South and West Yorkshire, 61,000 out of the West Midlands[25]. The South East has gained 230,000 people in the same period. Since 1994 an average of 14,000 more people have been moving south every year than in previous years[26]. The main reason is that there are simply more jobs in the South East. This is why house prices have jumped so much more in the South East than elsewhere in the last few years. It is fair to assume that a proportion of these incomers are churchgoers.

• One Report discussing these figures[27] does not give the social class of these migrants. Nor do the government's official figures on internal migration. But it might be assumed that the search for jobs, and therefore the greater proportion of movers, are those with a specific qualification to offer. It is well known that the church is "middle class", so it could be that more of these movers are Christian than in the general population, and this may partly explain why there are more Christians in the South East than in the population overall.

Figure 9 shows the percentage of the population attending church on Sunday by region for each of the years 1979, 1989 and 1998, using a common shading for the three maps. It is easy to see how sweeping the changes have been.

Figure 9a: Percentage of population attending church on Sunday 1979

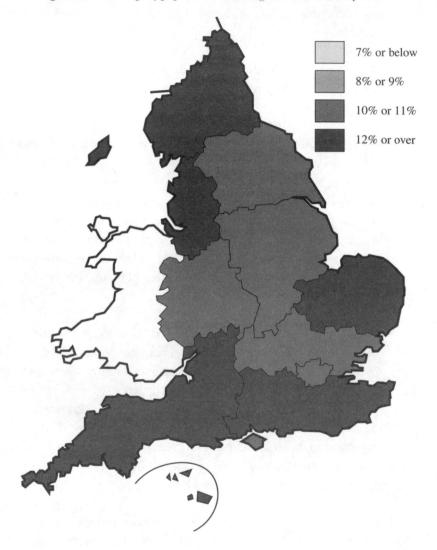

7% or below

8% or 9%

10% or 11%

12% or over

Figure 9b: Percentage of population attending church on Sunday 1989

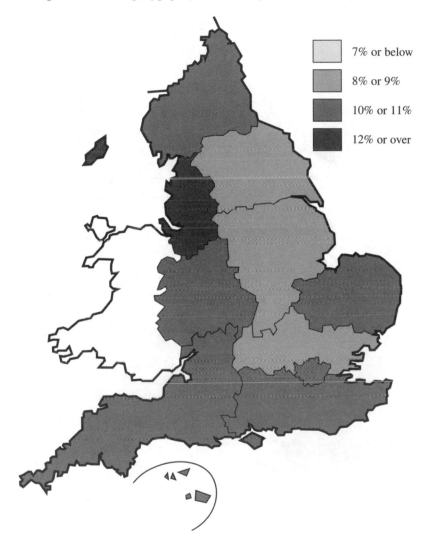

Figure 9c: Percentage of population attending church on Sunday 1998

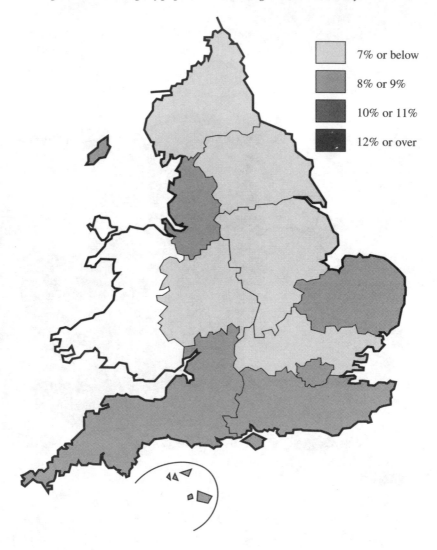

Roman Catholic Mass attendance by region

How have the different denominational groups fared across the country? We will look at these in terms of the three main building blocks to Sunday attendance the Roman Catholics, the Church of England and all the others. Table 17 gives the first of these.

Table 17: Roman Catholic Mass attendance by Region, 1979-1998

Region	1979	change	1989	change	1998
North	165,200	−15%	140,500	−37%	88,800
Yorks/Humberside	179,300	−17%	149,600	−42%	86,400
North West	526,100	−18%	430,900	−32%	292,800
East Midlands	97,800	−13%	84,700	−31%	58,600
West Midlands	218,400	− 6%	206,100	−37%	129,600
East Anglia	67,000	−16%	56,300	−41%	33,200
South East (North)	157,400	−20%	125,800	− 9%	114,500
Greater London	333,700	−12%	293,000	−19%	237,200
South East (South)	150,200	− 8%	137,600	− 9%	125,000
South West	95,900	− 5%	91,400	−30%	64,000
Total All England	**1,991,000**	**−14%**	**1,715,900**	**−28%**	**1,230,100**

Mass attendance has decreased in every part of England. However, while overall, as already noted, they declined twice as much in the 1990s as in the 1980s, this has not been repeated in every region. The West Midlands and the South West have fared much more badly with extremely sharp drops. The North, Yorks/Humberside, East Midlands and East Anglia have also had above average declines in the 1990s. The North West has dropped the most in numerical terms.

It is the South East which has dropped less, as for Sunday attendance as a whole. South East (North), whilst still decreasing, has in fact decreased less in the 1990s than in the 1980s, the only region to do so. It is also the one part of the country which saw a significant increase in the number of Roman Catholic priests in the 1970s and 1980s[28]: the Dioceses of Brentwood, Northampton and Westminster saw a collective increase of 8% in their number of priests 1963 to 1980 against a decline of 9% in the rest of England[29]. They have seen the same percentage decrease since 1980 however as other parts of the country, but because of their higher number in 1980 the proportionate decrease per thousand attending Mass is less – they have more priests per practising Catholic than elsewhere, not just suggesting that leadership is crucial but that the decline in the number of priests is also a significant reason in the Catholic Mass decline.

Anglican Sunday attendance by region

Table 18 gives the same breakdown as Table 17 but for the Anglicans.

Table 18: Anglican Sunday attendance by Region, 1979-1998

Region	1979	change	1989	change	1998
North	98,700	–23%	76,100	–27%	55,200
Yorks/Humberside	145,200	–26%	107,900	–22%	84,700
North West	219,900	–26%	162,800	–36%	104,800
East Midlands	141,000	–23%	108,400	–22%	84,700
West Midlands	169,900	–23%	131,300	–31%	91,100
East Anglia	97,000	–21%	76,300	–17%	63,600
South East (North)	174,800	–22%	135,500	–24%	103,600
Greater London	140,500	–30%	98,500	+3%	101,100
South East (South)	252,800	–24%	192,200	–20%	152,800
South West	231,200	–23%	177,300	–22%	139,000
Total All England	**1,671,000**	**–24%**	**1,266,300**	**–23%**	**980,600**

The pattern of decline of the Anglicans across the country is much more uniform than for the Roman Catholics, with many regions seeing their rate of decline in the 1990s much the same as in the 1980s. Exceptions are:

- The North West and West Midlands where the decline in the 1990s has been much worse than experienced in the 1980s, and

* Greater London, where far from having a decline in the
  1990s, the Church of England has seen increased attendance!

It is not clear why there should be such good success in Greater
London. The civil boundary of Greater London includes most of the
Diocese of London, the northern part of the Diocese of Southwark,
the extreme north western part of the Diocese of Rochester, and the
south western tip of the Diocese of Chelmsford. Because most of the
Diocese of London is within Greater London, its Diocesan figures
are often taken as speaking for the whole of London.

The growth reflected in Table 17 has been noticed and reported in
the church and secular press already[30]. These articles did not give
reasons for the increase though indicated that Christmas and Easter
communicants in the Diocese of London had also risen, Electoral
Rolls had increased, and the number of candidates for ordination
had gone up. A number of churches had undertaken courses in
evangelism, and giving for the Church Urban Fund to help the 40%
Urban Priority Areas had been over £10 million.

The Bishop of London, the Rt Rev Richard Chartres, said, "The
variety and texture of church life from which they are drawn is even
more encouraging." This presumably suggests that the increase is
seen across all churchmanships. No analysis, if undertaken by the
Diocese, has been made publicly available as to how far the increase
is due to the increased numbers attending the larger Anglican
churches like Holy Trinity, Brompton. Any growth clearly is good
news, and the figures must be seen in this light.

Free Churches' Sunday attendance by region

Table 19 gives the same regional breakdown as the previous two
Tables, for all the other denominations.

The pattern of change here is not uniform. The growth in East
Anglia and South East (South) in the 1980s was largely due to
increasing numbers in Independent and New Churches. In Greater

London it was also due to the growth in the Pentecostal churches, like Kensington Temple and Kingsway International which has grown from 200 to 6,000 in 6 years. This growth has continued in the 1990s among the New and Pentecostal churches in London, but there has also been growth among the Baptists (moderate), Orthodox (large), United Reformed (small) and Other Churches (large).

Table 19: Free Churches' Sunday attendance by Region, 1979-1998

Region	1979	change	1989	change	1998
North	101,400	– 5%	95,900	–15%	81,100
Yorks/Humberside	187,400	– 8%	172,100	–33%	115,300
North West	214,500	– 7%	199,400	–20%	159,200
East Midlands	145,400	– 7%	135,500	–13%	117,500
West Midlands	186,500	– 4%	179,300	–21%	142,300
East Anglia	86,700	+6%	91,800	–29%	65,600
South East (North)	188,200	– 2%	184,200	– 8%	168,800
Greater London	221,800	+16%	258,100	+8%	279,600
South East (South)	212,900	+1%	214,300	– 6%	201,200
South West	233,900	– 2%	230,200	–25%	173,400
Total All England	**1,779,000**	**– 1%**	**1,760,600**	**–15%**	**1,504,000**

Table 19 shows that:

- There has been substantial decline in both the South West and East Anglia, especially in the Independent and Methodist churches in both regions

- Continuing, and now substantial, decline also in the Yorks/Humberside region, again especially Methodist, but also Pentecostal

- Declines in the North, North West, East and West Midlands and South East (North) regions have been 2, 3 or 4 times the rate of the 1980s in the 1990s mostly among the Independent and Methodist churches, though also the URC in the East Midlands and South East (North)

• The same factors have caused the decline in the South East (South) region, not offset by growth among the Baptist, Pentecostal and New Churches.

Regional Sunday attendance by churchmanship

Table 20 shows the change in Sunday attendance between 1989 and 1998 for the evangelicals and all other churchmanships.

It is immediately obvious that the non-evangelicals have declined much more than the evangelicals in the 1990s, in fact, ten times as much. The non-evangelical decline is fairly uniform across the country, slightly worse in the West Midlands (extra large Catholic decline), and slightly better in South East (North) (large Anglo-Catholic growth) and in Greater London (large Low Church growth). That Greater London dropped least of all corroborates the Bishop of London's comment that in his Diocese he was seeing growth across the "variety and texture of church life".

Table 20: Regional Sunday attendance by churchmanship, 1989-1998

Region	Evangelicals			All other churchmanships		
	1989	change	1998	1989	change	1998
North	73,900	–19%	59,800	238,600	–31%	165,300
Yorks/Humberside	120,900	–29%	86,200	308,700	–35%	200,200
North West	169,300	– 5%	160,600	623,800	–36%	396,200
East Midlands	106,000	– 4%	102,100	222,600	–29%	158,700
West Midlands	134,100	+7%	143,400	382,600	–43%	219,600
East Anglia	80,000	–12%	70,300	144,400	–36%	92,100
South East (North)	161,100	– 5%	152,600	284,200	–18%	234,300
Greater London	216,800	+18%	255,800	432,800	–16%	362,100
South East (South)	190,200	+10%	209,500	353,900	–24%	269,500
South West	178,100	–15%	151,000	320,800	–30%	225,400
Total All England	**1,430,400**	**– 3%**	**1,391,300**	**3,312,400**	**–30%**	**2,323,400**

Evangelical change is uneven. There is almost as much loss among evangelicals as non-evangelicals in Yorks/Humberside, the only region for which this is so. The same trend may be observed in the

South West, although not as much. In both cases the cause is the same – the huge drop in the number of Methodists, many of whom classify themselves as Broad Evangelicals. The decline in the North is also because of the drop in the number of Broad Evangelicals, but this time it is not the Methodists so much as the Anglicans.

The North West, East Midlands and South East (North) almost held their own in the 1990s, partly because of the strength of the Baptist, New or Pentecostal churches in these regions. It was these denominations which caused the actual growth seen in the West Midlands, Greater London and South East (South). Both the Methodist and Pentecostals declined in East Anglia, and the other evangelicals could not make up the difference.

Severe decline

The headlines continue to be dramatic. The *Sunday Times* in July 1999 for example said "Future of C of E in the balance as attendance falls"[31], but others are equally strident. "Something is seriously wrong with the church. People are leaving it in droves," wrote Rev Dr Derek Tidball, the Principal of London Bible College[32]. "The church is in trouble and doesn't know it," said Mike Riddell, a New Zealander attending a Brainstormer Conference in the UK[33]. Such comments could be multiplied.

It is clear the situation has become worse in the 1990s than in the 1980s. Has it deteriorated uniformly during the 1990s? There is little direct evidence and the ECAS survey cannot help since it only measured the 1998 figures. There was no equivalent survey in the mid-1990s.

As mentioned in the previous chapter, there was one major event in the 1990s which may have caused some of the problem – Margaret Thatcher's passing of the Sunday Trading Law in 1994 which allowed shops to open on Sundays. I believe this one Act and the consequent increased secularisation of Sunday has impacted church attendance irrevocably, and is part of the reason why Christianity may be churchless by 2010, and in that sense, could bleed to death.

SUMMARY

1 More than a million people stopped attending church on Sunday in the 9 years 1989 to 1998.

2 If the rate of decline continues there could be only a small percentage in church in a generation's time – the church could bleed to death.

3 The institutional churches have declined more than the non-institutional.

4 The Church of England and the Roman Catholic church have each seen Sunday attendance drop between 40 and 50% in the last two decades.

5 Of the non-institutional churches only the Baptists and New Churches have grown in the 1990s, the first by only a little. Part of the New Church growth however has been through Independent churches joining one of their streams.

6 There are 16,000 churches in England with a usual Sunday attendance of 50 or fewer. 3,000 churches have average congregations of over 300 people, 2,000 of them Roman Catholic.

7 The Church of England had the smallest average congregations of any denomination in England in 1998 with 60 on a normal Sunday; the New Churches the largest with 138 after the Roman Catholics with 326.

8 Church attendance has not dropped uniformly across the country, with the South East, and especially Greater London, seeing far less decline than elsewhere. This is perhaps because of continuing migration to the south east from other regions, and partly because of the growth of several very large churches in London.

9 Evangelicals have declined at one-tenth of the rate of non-evangelicals; in 1998 they were three-eighths, 37%, of all churchgoers.

10 The culture change in English society caused by the Sunday Shopping Act in 1994 could account for some of the severe decline in churchgoing.

NOTES

1. Report in the *Daily Telegraph*, 14th December 1998.
2. Quoted in *Idea,* Information Service of the German Evangelical Alliance, English Edition, Number 21, 3rd November 1998, Page 4, based on survey by the Barna Research Group.
3. Quoted in *Religion Watch,* Volume 14, Number 5, March 1999, Page 6.
4. Edwards, Very Rev David L, *A Concise History of English Christianity,* 1998, HarperCollins, London, Page 166.
5. Brierley, Dr Peter, *Future Church,* 1998, Monarch Publications, Crowborough, East Sussex.
6. *Prospects for Scotland 2000,* Report of the 1994 Scottish Church Census, Rev Fergus MacDonald and Peter Brierley, National Bible Society of Scotland, Edinburgh, and Christian research, London, 1995.
7. Report in *Church Times,* 7th February 1997, Page 1.
8. Report in the *Daily Telegraph,* 11th June 1999, Page 13.
9. Mentioned in discussion at the Denton Conference on Implicit Religion, May 1999.
10. A 1992 survey reported in *Quadrant,* Christian Research, London, January 1994, Page 5.
11. Listed for example in Brierley, Dr Peter, editor, *Religious Trends* No 2, 2000/2001, Christian Research and HarperCollins, London, 1999, Pages 9.12-14.
12. Love, Mervyn, editor, *The Body Book,* 7th edition, 1998, Pioneer, Surrey.
13. This percentage takes into account the "white" component of "other denominations".
14. Op cit (Item 11), Page 9.9.
15. The 1979 and 1989 figures are revised higher estimates, with the difference taken out of the "Other denominations" figure.
16. Op cit (Item 11), Page 9.27.
17. Op cit (Item 11), Page 9.29-31.
18. Paper *"From Religion to Ethics: Quaker amillennialism"* given by Ben Pink Dandelion at the British Sociological Association Conference, Bristol, 4th April 1997.
19. For example, by Gerald Coates at the 1992 Challenge 2000 Conference for new and growing churches.
20. Given in Brierley, Peter, editor, *Prospects for the Nineties,* MARC Europe, London, 1991, Page 21, etc.
21. Article *"7 Trends affecting you"* by Schaller, Rev Lyle E, parish consultant for the Yokefellow Institute, Illinois, United States, in *Leadership* magazine, Spring 1998, Page 97.

22. Ibid.
23. A survey form developed by Christian Research and available for individual church use.
24. Wakefield, Rev Dr Gavin, PhD Thesis, *Finding a Church,* March 1998, available from the author at St John's College, Durham.
25. *Population Estimates,* Mid-1998, Series PE No 1, Office for National Statistics, 1999.
26. See for example report in the *Daily Telegraph,* 25th June 1999.
27. Holmans, Professor and Simpson, Merron, *Low Demand: Separating Fact from Fiction,* 1999, Joseph Rowntree Foundation and Chartered Institute of Housing.
28. Op cit (Item 11), Figure 8.9.1.
29. Op cit (Item 11), Figure 8.9.2 and 8.10.
30. See for example the article in the *Church of England Newspaper* on 12th March 1999, or *Church Times* of the same date, both of which were preceded by an article in the *Daily Telegraph* of 8th March 1999.
31. Report by Chris Morgan in the *Sunday Times,* 11th July 1999.
32. Article *"Where is the Church going?"* by Rev Dr Derek Tidball in the *European Christian Bookstore Journal,* March/April 1999, Page 3.
33. Article *"The Church is in trouble"* by Mike Riddell in *Youthwork,* June 1999, Page 25.

3: *Regular? At Festivals!*

At a 1993 Christmas carol service I sat behind someone I hadn't seen before, and asked if it was their first time. "Oh, we come regularly to this church," they said, "every Christmas!" They came for a real reason – their son had been tragically killed in his early 20s just before Christmas, and the church had taken the funeral which they had greatly appreciated. Each year they came to remember their son, and to say "thank you" to the church.

Between the "twicers" who attend twice on Sunday, and such "Christmas-specials" lies a whole range of attendance. An Australian Baptist colleague, Glenda Wheldon, once said, "I always thought 'C of E' meant 'Christmas and Easter only'"!

One of the more interesting developments during the final decade of the 20th century is that the frequency with which people attend church has begun to vary much more than in previous decades. In the 1970s if you asked someone "Do you go to church?" and they said YES, you could virtually take it for granted that it meant every week. Not so in the 1980s and especially not in the 1990s!

Existing information

In the same week in February 1997 when the Church of England announced a 3% drop in the number attending services, the largest for 20 years, an article appeared in the *Church Times* by the Rector of West Monkton in the Diocese of Bath and Wells[1]. He said that

71

when he first went to his church there were 150 people associated with it (the community). These divided into three groups of 50: the first attended every week, the second came once a month, and the third came only at Easter and Christmas. Ignoring the last group, the average weekly attendance was 50 + 25% of 50 = 62 people.

Ten years later, the first group had reduced to 40 people largely through death, the second group had expanded to 60, and the third had remained much the same. His weekly attendance was therefore 40 + 25% of 60 = 55. So his attendance had reduced by the order of 10% but the number of people connected with his church is still the same. This kind of situation can be replicated across most of the country.

What measurements of churchgoing frequency exist? The British Social Attitudes (BSA) Survey collects such information. In 1997, the latest year for which it has been published[2], it found that 12% of the population claimed to attend weekly, 2% fortnightly, 6% monthly, 12% every six months, 5% once a year, 4% less than once a year, 24% never who were nevertheless "religious", and 35% who never went because they weren't "religious". Figures from the 1990 European Values Study[3] found 13% of the population attended weekly, 10% monthly, 12% at Christmas and Easter, 8% once a year, and 57% never (not distinguishing the last two groups of the BSA study). These two sets of figures from entirely different sources are close, but suffer from the huge disadvantage that the percentage claiming to attend church every week is way ahead of that actually measured.

In Australia the 1991 National Church Life Survey[4] puts 11% of the population in church on an average Sunday, perhaps a further 2% would attend less than frequently[5], a total of 13%. When the Pope visited Australia in November 1996, his sermon at Sydney stressed the need to reach those who had heard the Gospel but who "no longer respond". "I am thinking, " he said, "of those baptised in the faith who are no longer actively present in the Church. They are of many different types, and the reasons for their absence from the community of Christ's faithful are also many."[6] In the United States people are also attending church less frequently.[7]

Church of England experiments

Two key studies have been carried out by the Anglican Dioceses of Ripon (now Ripon and Leeds) and of Wakefield. In Ripon, for example, a head count was made in 110 out of the 159 parishes of everyone attending church during a 4-week period April/May 1998. This showed that in total 27,947 individuals came to church at least once, compared to an average Sunday attendance of 11,548, a ratio of 2.42 times as many. A third of those who attended, 34%, in total 9,585 people, came because they were attending an occasional service such as a funeral or wedding, but even if these are excluded the resulting ratio of 1.59 shows that many more people are involved with church than actually appear on any particular Sunday[8].

Similar findings were observed in Wakefield. When Rev Stephen Cottrell, now a missioner with the Archbishop's evangelistic initiative *Springboard,* but formerly a vicar in the Wakefield Diocese, was explaining the results at a meeting considering church statistics as a "tool for mission" in October 1998, he said these kinds of results were "of most value at parish level revealing patterns of attendance that raised questions about communication, pastoral care, and the effective use of ministry."[9]

Another spokesman for the Church of England has said, "Our present statistics do not give a clear picture and for a long time we have been looking for a way to give a more accurate picture"[10]. Under Rt Rev Nigel McCulloch, the Bishop of Wakefield, a Working party has been set up to look into this issue.

The survey question

"Seven times a day I praise you"[11], says the Psalmist. What kind of worship participation should we therefore consider? Julian

Cummins, a director of Avista management consultants, who is closely involved with the church, wrote, "If we are to take maximum possible participation in worship in England it is probably 7 x 365 x 45 million. But this is obviously absurd – we would be seeking to measure the uncountable level of engagement with God in private prayer and worship. But this uncountable total is actually what we are seeking to encourage, not attendance at selected services at church."[12]

He went on to argue that whatever benchmark we use is necessarily arbitrary. That is true, but we need to have one so that year on year comparisons may be made, and also one which will enable comparisons across different denominations. Hence the continued use of membership even though fewer people today think membership is important, and each denomination measures it differently.

Ascertaining the frequency with which people attended church was one of the major priorities behind the ECAS study. It would allow the Diocesan experimental figures to be compared across the country and across the different denominations. The question asked the minister or other person completing the form to estimate the approximate numbers of the total adult congregation who attend Sunday services weekly, fortnightly, monthly, quarterly or twice a year, but counting those who might attend twice on a Sunday only once. The question also asked respondents to indicate if they were a visitor or it was the first time they had attended this particular church.

It was appreciated this was not an easy question, and to help respondents a slip was provided, which by photocopying, enabled individuals in each congregation to indicate their personal frequency of attendance. 41% of respondents passed these slips out; as their answers did not differ significantly from the 59% who estimated the answers, we assume that their estimates were reasonable[13]. Estimators tended to put one person per 50 attending weekly as attending fortnightly and one person in 50 as attending monthly.

It is reasonable to assume that if there are a body of churchgoers who only go every fortnight that on an average Sunday half of these will be present. Likewise of those who only come once a month, on any given Sunday a quarter will turn up. It may be that such people come for communion once a month, or to a family service. Over the whole spectrum of services and denominations across the land, in the absence of information to the contrary, it is reasonable to assume that communion or family services are held in equal numbers on every Sunday.

Does the same line of reasoning work for those who come quarterly or twice a year? Almost certainly not. On some of the forms where the figures were actual counts, the respondent added the words "estimated" for the quarterly and twice a year figures. The majority of those who come twice a year will probably attend over Christmas or Easter, as my Australian friend suggested. Hence it seems unreasonable to take the percentage who said they come twice a year as being equally distributed across six months and that 1/26th of them happened to be present on September's Survey Sunday. And yet some obviously were, as they said so! We have assumed that the number who said they come twice a year are half those in this category, and those who said they come quarterly a quarter.

Visitors

One person in 20, 5%, indicated he/she was a visitor or a first-comer. We cannot divide the numbers between these two groups. It is of course quite possible that some of the visitors were normally regular churchgoers at other churches, and they were simply in another church on the survey Sunday because they were visiting a friend or relative. The month chosen for the survey, September 1998, was not a prime holiday month, but almost certainly nevertheless, some of the visitors would also have been holiday makers.

How far those saying they were visitors were really such is not known either; in some surveys we have undertaken of individual church congregations we have found a few people who have been coming to a church regularly for years still think of themselves as a "visitor" because they have not integrated into the church as much as they would like for whatever reason.

Whatever the correctness of this 5% figure, and however it is made up, the total number has been excluded from the overall estimating of the frequency with which people come to church, that is, the remaining numbers in this chapter are based on 95% of Sunday churchgoers.

It may, however, be worth pausing to look at the variations in the percentage of visitors across the three dimensions of this survey denomination, churchmanship and region and these are given in the next Table.

Table 21: Percentage of visitors (V) in 1998

Denomination	V %	Churchmanship	V %	Region	V %
Anglican	8	Anglo-Catholic	5	North	7
Baptist	4	Broad	12	Yorks/Humberside	9
Catholic	1	Catholic	2	North West	4
Independent	4	Evan: Broad	7	East Midlands	9
Methodist	8	Evan: Mainstream	4	West Midlands	4
New Church	4	Evan: Charismatic	5	East Anglia	4
Orthodox	1	Evangelical:Total	5	S E (North)	5
Pentecostal	4	Liberal	8	Gr London	4
URC	6	Low Church	8	S E (South)	3
Others	3	Others	5	South West	7

This Table shows that Anglicans and Methodists had the most visitors in a normal service, and Roman Catholics and the Orthodox the least. Those who described themselves as broad, liberal or low church theologically had the most, and mainstream evangelicals and Catholics the least. More visitors were apparent in Yorks/ Humberside and East Midlands churches, and fewest in the counties in the South East (South) region.

Frequency of attendance

The percentage of people who came to church ...

- Twice a week was   12%
- Weekly   46%
- Fortnightly   11%
- Monthly   9%
- Quarterly   5%
- Twice a year   17%.

Thus 58%, the total of the first two figures, represents the percentage of churchgoers who attend every week. 42% therefore attend less frequently. But since the survey asked for attendance on an average Sunday it would only "catch" half of those who attend fortnightly and a quarter of those who go monthly. The actual number of people who attend church is therefore much greater than the numbers given in the last chapter which just looked at attendance on an average Sunday. Adding in these extra people and expressing the results as a percentage of the population, we get:

- 7.5% attend weekly
- 8.3% attend fortnightly
- 10.2% attend monthly
- 11.3% attend quarterly
- 12.6% attend twice a year

It would be nice to complete this sequence of those who attend church once a year. This question was not asked so the data must come from elsewhere. Dr Clive Field of Birmingham University Library has helpfully collated the various Gallup and other like polls who have asked people over the last 40 years whether they attended church at Christmas[14]. Averaging these various results, 35% said they went in the 1960s, 36% in the 1970s, 28% in the 1980s and 31%

in the 1990s[15]. However what people say they do and what they actually do are not the same. The percentages of church attendance from the British Social Attitudes Survey were roughly twice that of the actual[16]. Applying the same proportion to the 1990s Christmas figure we get as the actual percentage of the population:

- 16.2% attend once a year

This is over 8 million people in England who come inside a church at least once a year. In addition there will be many more who attend baptisms or christenings, marriages and funerals whose numbers are not known. In Australia in 1997, 29% had attended a baptism, 37% a wedding and 44% a funeral[17]; it is likely similar percentages would have done so in the UK. It must be remembered, though, that the present availability of wedding solemnisation in a variety of locations other than a church may result in fewer people entering a church building for a special occasion. In addition, funeral services often take place in a Crematorium chapel, not a church.

The 16.2% is 2.2 times the 7.5% weekly figure, and gives a kind of "multiplier" to move from one to the other. So for every 5 churchgoers in church on an average Sunday there are another 6 who sometimes come. In other words more than as many people again attend church in a year as on an average Sunday. In terms of the media's word "reach", the church's reach is to a sixth of the population vis-a-vis building or congregation contact.

Some will say this is massaging the figures to get as impressive a figure as one can, and to put as good a face on declining Sunday attendance as possible. Not at all! It is important to be realistic and see how many people come and how often.

What is a reasonable figure for the measurement of frequency? The most generally used time period is a month, and for the church to focus on "a shorter time period is to deliberately and unnecessarily underestimate our participation compared to other things in society"[18]. On that basis we should say that just over 10% of the pop-

ulation comes to church at least once a month. It is strongly suggested that churches use a month to average attendance, especially as
weekly and fortnightly attendance is so variable.

Churchgoing more popular than football!

8 million people may attend church sometime during the year, but
what is the total number of attendances? On the above figures they
come to 213 million, which is more than 8 times the 25 million[19] who
attend football each year! It is a pity the church doesn't get 8 times
the media coverage given to football!

These figures also mean that each churchgoer attends church on
average about 25 times a year. That is, people who go to church
attend once a fortnight on average.

Variation in the frequency of churchgoing

It would be interesting to know how the figures given above have
changed. Unfortunately the relevant questions were not put in the
1979 or 1989 studies, though they both asked the percentage who
attended church twice a week. In 1985 this was 16%, in 1989 14%,
and had dropped to 12% in 1998.

The 1979 English Church Census asked for figures averaged over a
month, so the overall percentage of 11.7% of the population could be
taken as a monthly figure. Against this figure the 1998 10.2% seems a
much smaller decline. The drop in actual numbers is 375,000 people,
which is 37% of the decline in the 1990s. This could suggest that just
over a third of the decline we have seen in Sunday attendance is due
to the change in people's attendance habits rather than people leaving
the church per se.

This is important. If we forget for a moment that a third have
changed frequency, then the decline in the 1990s would be 14%
against a drop of 13% in the 1980s. These are effectively the same
when the potential error in measurement is taken into account. So

the decline in the 1980s has continued in the 1990s at the same rate, and it is the major factor of change of frequency that has caused the 1990s dip to be so much more severe. It is this frequency change which is the new dimension to churchgoing in the 1990s (or non-churchgoing!).

Churchgoing frequency by denomination

How do the figures for frequency of attendance vary be denomination? Table 22 gives this information, which is illustrated in Figure 10. The final column gives a "ratio" figure the number by which the weekly attendance should be multiplied to give an estimate of attendance at least twice a year.

Table 22: Frequency of church attendance per year by denomination, 1998

Denomination	Twice a week %	Weekly %	Fortnightly %	Monthly %	Quarterly %	Twice a year %	Total (≈100%)	Ratio
Anglican	7	39	14	12	6	22	980,500	2.2
Baptist	22	51	10	6	3	7	277,600	1.4
Roman Catholic	7	57	6	5	3	22	1,230,100	1.6
Independent	31	43	9	6	3	8	161,600	1.4
Methodist	14	47	13	10	5	11	379,700	1.6
New Churches	26	53	10	5	3	3	230,500	1.3
Orthodox	5	10	9	11	4	61	25,200	6.7
Pentecostal	33	39	8	9	3	8	214,600	1.4
United Reformed	7	52	14	11	7	9	121,700	1.7
Other denoms.	25	41	9	10	5	10	93,100	1.5
OVERALL	**12**	**46**	**11**	**9**	**5**	**17**	**3,714,700**	**1.7**

The Orthodox have the rather unique distinction of almost two-thirds of their congregations coming only twice a year! Christmas and Easter, especially the latter with its strong resurrection emphasis, are the main times when the Orthodox gather.

Figure 10: Frequency of Sunday church attendance by denomination, 1998

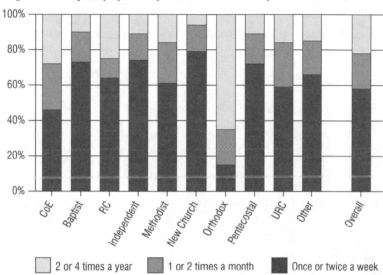

After the Orthodox, the Church of England is the only denomination whose weekly attendance, once or twice, is less than 50%, and the only denomination with a ratio greater than 2. In other words, the Anglicans have the smallest proportion of committed people, if commitment is measured by churchgoing frequency. Strongest are the New Churches where virtually four-fifths, 79%, attend every week, followed by the Independent churches, Baptists and Pentecostals.

Those with the largest proportion attending 2 to 4 times a year after the Orthodox (65%) are the Anglicans (28%) followed closely by the Roman Catholics (25%), and then the Methodists and URC (both 16%).

"I've based today's hymns on last month's attendance figures."

Churchgoing frequency by churchmanship

Table 23 gives similar information broken down by churchmanship, and Figure 11 reflects this.

Table 23: Churchgoing frequency by churchmanship, 1998

Churchmanship	Twice a week %	Weekly %	Fortnightly %	Monthly %	Quarterly %	Twice a year %	Total (=100%)	Ratio
Anglo-Catholic	9	41	12	13	6	19	177,600	2.0
Broad	8	42	12	11	6	21	352,400	2.0
Catholic	7	56	7	5	3	22	980,000	1.6
Evangelical	22	47	10	7	4	10	1,391,300	1.4
Liberal	9	40	13	12	5	21	425,500	2.0
Low Church	8	46	14	10	5	17	275,400	1.9
Others	13	46	9	7	4	21	112,500	1.7
Broad evangelical	11	44	13	10	6	16	217,900	1.8
Mainstream evang.	25	46	9	7	3	10	645,500	1.4
Charismatic evang.	24	48	11	6	3	8	527,900	1.4
OVERALL	**12**	**46**	**11**	**9**	**5**	**17**	**3,714,700**	**1.7**

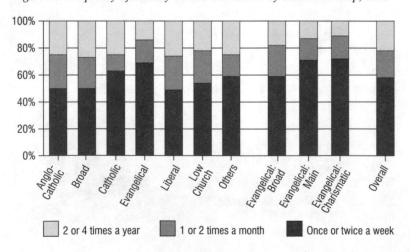

Figure 11: Frequency of Sunday church attendance by churchmanship, 1998

The Evangelicals have the highest percentage going on a weekly basis, 69%, mainly because of the charismatic and mainstream commitment to weekly attendance, followed by the Catholics (63%).

The Liberals have the smallest going weekly (49%), followed closely by the Anglo-Catholics and Broad churchgoers (both 50%).

The percentages represented in Figures 10 and 11 are given broken down by region in *Religious Trends* No 2.[20]

Churchgoing frequency by region

How does the frequency of churchgoing vary by region? Table 24 gives the basic figures, and Figure 12 is a map showing the percentage attending at least once a week.

There is a much greater homogeneity of frequency of attendance by region. The North has the greatest percentage going weekly (68%), followed by Yorks/Humberside and the North West (both 64%), with the South West (56%) and the East Midlands (54%) the lowest. In other words, this change of frequency is a national phenomenon not a rural/urban one.

Table 24: Churchgoing frequency by region, 1998

Region	Twice a week %	Weekly %	Fortnightly %	Monthly %	Quarterly %	Twice a year %	Total (=100%)	Ratio
North	11	57	8	7	3	14	225,100	1.5
Yorks/Humberside	14	50	10	8	4	14	286,400	1.6
North West	12	52	8	7	5	16	556,800	1.6
East Midlands	11	43	11	11	5	19	260,800	1.9
West Midlands	14	49	9	7	5	16	363,000	1.6
East Anglia	20	40	10	8	5	17	162,400	1.7
S East (North)	12	47	11	8	5	17	386,900	1.7
Greater London	12	50	10	8	4	16	617,900	1.6
South East (South)	13	47	10	9	5	16	479,000	1.7
South West	12	44	10	8	5	21	376,400	1.8
OVERALL	**12**	**46**	**11**	**9**	**5**	**17**	**3,714,700**	**1.7**

Why has churchgoing decreased?

This question is linked with the question of why people leave church. The change in numbers analysed thus far is based on net changes, that is to say, of gains less losses. These broader figures are less robustly researched. But from a series of surveys across different denominations undertaken by Christian Research in the early 1990s[21], some of that broad picture may be discerned.

In the 1980s and 1990s 1.6 million people have started going to church, about 2.5% of the population. At the same time we have lost 2.8 million, just over a fifth through death, and about four-fifths for other, perhaps preventable, reasons. Of these, almost half are because of the changing frequency of attendance. Thus the real loss from a worshipping congregation relates to the 40% who left over these two decades but who might have stayed. This is what is causing the church as a whole to lose more than we gain, and the rate of loss is accelerating.

Of the 40% who leave, about half are "recycling", that is, they are in the process of moving to another church but haven't quite got there yet, as it takes time to find a new place of worship. Many of these are likely to have said they were "visitors" on the ECAS form. Part of this process is often a change of denomination as well as change of location.[22]

Of the other 20%, perhaps a fifth will come back again, usually after an average of 8 or 10 years away[23]. The other 16% won't. Philip Richter and Leslie Francis, respectively Methodist and Anglican educational researchers, in an important study of why people leave church, *Gone but not Forgotten*,[24] found the main reasons for leaving were, in order, unfulfilled expectations, changes in life circumstances, and loss of faith.

One key statistic the authors found was that 92% of people who left the church were not asked by anyone in their church why their attendance was dropping off. Half of these, 45%, said they would have re-considered returning, but the door of opportunity passed.

Figure 12: Those attending church at least once or twice a week, 1998

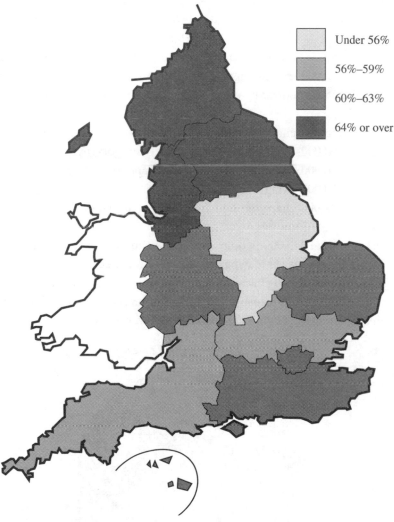

Under 56%

56%–59%

60%–63%

64% or over

This suggests the importance of vigilance in churches, and maybe an attendance rota would help identify such people. We were sent some examples with returned forms. They were word processed and easily completed each Sunday. One church included a figure of the number of regulars who might be expected to come each Sunday!

Using the above percentages and earlier research, then in the 1990s, across all the churches in England, the gross figures of attendance change are:

    +60,000   outside people joining the churches ("conversions")
    +60,000   ex-churchgoers rejoining the church
   +355,000   changing churches (mostly because they move)

    −355,000   changing churches
     −60,000   other churchgoers leaving temporarily
    −250,000   churchgoers leaving permanently
    −310,000   dying
    −530,000   changing their frequency of attendance

These total 475,000 people joining the church and 1,505,000 leaving. The reasons for leaving are shown in the piechart in Figure 13. The numbers leaving because of change of frequency are larger than the earlier figure because these are based on gross figures - some of those joining the church will also not attend weekly.

Figure 13: Why people leave the church

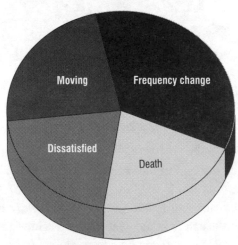

Decreasing frequency the key reason

It may thus be seen that the change in churchgoing frequency is the major reason why church attendance is dropping so greatly at the moment. It is therefore important to consider reasons why this may be so.

The Diocese of Oxford worked with Gallup poll to interview 1,016 people. Why didn't they come to church?

- "The biggest reason why people don't come to church is that they are too busy on Sunday mornings!"[25] This was true even for 35% of regular worshippers. Social changes have brought competition to the Sunday slot.

- The church services were uninviting. "Boring" and "old-fashioned" were quoted alike by regulars, occasionals and non-churchgoers.[26] They were hard to follow and had hymns not everyone recognised. This was an Anglican survey so the difficult services may be less true in non-liturgical churches. Shorter services were desired (the time factor again).

- The sermons did not teach enough basic Christianity. It is interesting that one of the reasons why the Alpha course has proved popular is that it has done just this, and church people often attend as well as non-church people. "The position of the modern believer is ... that, while he may still believe, he cannot avoid the knowledge that many people (including many people like him) believe other things"[27] (or nothing at all).

- Not enough involvement with the community. Relationships are especially important to the current, post-modern, generation. Helping people through service with the local community can encourage people to come and stay in church. To put it bluntly, they feel they are wanted and valued.

- Non-churchgoers don't "experiment" with church as it is seen as not being relevant. In 1980 about 3% of the population attended church "to see what it was like", but this had shrunk to 1% in 1990[28]. It is probably about 0.5% now. While it may be true in Britain as in the United States that "spirituality is a mile wide but an inch deep"[29] people do not associate churchgoing with spirituality(!).

The dissatisfaction with church services is evident in other contexts also. A snap poll on the Ship of Fools website for example found 49% replying YES to the question "Remembering the church service you went to on Sunday, would you have been better off staying at home?"![30] It is hard to keep being innovative, especially as students now say something is "traditional" after as little as two years.

In some contexts there is also a weariness of the committed. One letter writer said, "It doesn't say much about devotion to God if we go to church only when we are 'on duty' as sidesman, lesson-reader, etc. To be known as a regular churchgoer is a real act of Christian witness."[31] Some only go to church when they are doing something (which may be true of some clergy also!).

There are perhaps two other reasons why people tend to leave:

- A lack of willingness by the church leaders to take risks in new initiatives. This may be seen in the reducing number of church plants, but is true generally and not just in this particular.

- A loss of confidence by church leaders, ordained and lay, especially when in their own families their children do not follow them in the faith.

Canon Geoffrey Walker, Diocesan Missioner in the Bath and Wells Diocese, studied Canadian church life during a sabbatical. His summary of the missionary task of local Canadian churches is true of Britain also[32]. He distinguished four types of people:

- The lapsed, who are high on God but low on the church;
- Committed participants, regular attenders who are both high on God and high on the church;
- Participants, who are high on the church but low on God, characterised by low levels of church involvement outside worship;
- The conditional, who are moving from being participants into becoming the lapsed and are characterised by decreasing frequency of attendance and participation.

Perhaps the question to be asked is, "How do we identify the members of our congregation by these four criteria?"

SUMMARY

1 Church of England experiments found that up to 2.4 times more people attended church than came weekly.

2 5% of churchgoers described themselves as Visitors, especially Anglicans and Methodists.

3 58% of churchgoers attend at least once a week, 69% fortnightly and 78% monthly.

4 10% of the population attend church at least once a month, and 16% once a year.

5 One-third of the decline in attendance in the 1990s has been because of the change in frequency of attendance.

6 Orthodox attend least frequently, followed by the Anglicans.

7 New Churches have the highest attendance frequency, followed by the Baptists, Independents and Pentecostals.

8 The frequency of churchgoing is much the same in all parts of the country, though is strongest in the North.

9 People are too busy to come to church – and services are not always inviting.

10 The image of churchgoing is poor and involvement with the community needs to be greater.

NOTES

1. *Newcomers hidden behind the numbers,* article by Preb Rodney Schofield, Rector of West Monkton, Bath & Wells, Church Times, 7th February 1997.
2. *British Social Attitudes,* National Community Research Centre.
3. Taken from figures given by Dr Grace Davie at the Sociology of Religion Study Group meeting of the British Sociological Association in April 1997, which in turn were adapted from Ashford and Timms book of 1992.
4. Kaldor, Dr Peter, et al, *Winds of Change,* 1994, Lancer, New South Wales, Australia, Page 263.
5. Ibid. Page 106.
6. Report in *The Times,* 27th November 1996.
7. Report in *Idea,* Information Service of the German Evangelical Alliance, English Edition No 21, 3rd November 1998 of study by George Barna.
8. Report in *Religion Watch,* September 1998, Page 6.
9. Letter from Raymond Tongue, Statistics Unit, Church House, of 20th January 1999, which included a report of the October 1998 meeting.
10. Report in the *Daily Telegraph,* 13th January 1998.
11. Psalm 119 verse 164.
12. Personal fax from Julian Cummins of 14th September 1999.
13. The actual results were as follows, all with 20 degrees of freedom: Twice weekly $t=0.55$, $P=0.294$; Weekly $t=2.50$; $P=0.011$; Fortnightly $t=2.86$; $P=0.005$; Monthly $t=2.35$; $P=0.015$; Quarterly $t=1.28$; $P=0.108$; Twice a year $t=0.43$; $P=0.348$. These are all non-significant at the $P<0.001$ level, and all except one at the $P<0.010$ level.
14. Article *"When a Child is Born",* Field, Dr Clive, in *Modern Believing,* Journal of the Modern Churchpeople's Union, Volume 40, Number 3, 1999, Pages 29-40.
15. These figures are graphed in Brierley, Dr Peter, editor, *Religious Trends* No 2, 2000/2001, 1999, HarperCollins and Christian Research, London, Table 5.6.2.
16. See *Religious Trends* No 1, 1998/1999, 1997, Paternoster Publishing, Carlisle, and Christian Research, London, Tables 2.12.4 and 2.13.1 where the average of the latter over the former for 1985, 1990 and 1995 is 1.92.
17. Kaldor, Dr Peter, *Build My Church,* 1999, Open Book Publishers, New South Wales, Australia, Page 18.
18. Op cit. (Item 12).
19. Press Release of CPO, Worthing, September 1999.
20. Op cit. (Item 15), Section 12.
21. The detail is available in Brierley, Dr Peter, *Changing Churches,* Leaders

Briefing No 3, 1996, Christian Research, London.
22. Wakefield, Dr Gavin, *Finding a Church,* 1998, available from the author at St John's College, Durham. He found for example 35% of Anglicans changed denomination in moving.
23. Gibbs, Professor Eddie, *Winning Them Back,* 1993, Monarch, Crowborough, East Sussex.
24. Richter, Philip and Francis, Professor Leslie, 1998, *Gone but not Forgotten,* Darton, Longman and Todd, London, Page 137
25. Report by Richard Thomas in *The Door,* May 1999, Page 10.
26. Report by Sarah Meyrick in the *Church Times,* 30th April 1999.
27. Berger, Peter, *The Heretical Imperative,* 1980, Collins, London, explaining the title of the book, quoted in Bruce, Professor Steve, Conservative Protestant Politics, 1998, Oxford University Press, Oxford.
28. Op cit (Item 16), Table 2.2.
29. Kinnaman, David, Barna Research Group, *Religion Watch,* Volume 14 Number 5, March 1999, Page 6.
30. Report by Pat Ashworth in the *Church Times,* 9th July 1999.
31. Letter from L J Carey, Chippenham, Wiltshire in the *Church Times,* 25th September 1998.
32. Article by Canon Geoffrey Walker in *Anvil,* Volume 16, Number 1, 1999, Pages 19-29.

4: One Generation from Extinction!

When addressing bishops, missionaries and other members of the clergy at a meeting of the Church of England Board of Mission at Swanwick, Derbyshire in March 1999 Archbishop George Carey said "the church is one generation away from extinction"[1]. As the full text of his talk makes clear, the Archbishop had no special analysis to back his comment for he was primarily using the phrase for emphasis. Unless we reach the next generation, the church is always one generation from extinction; mission must always be our primary task and goal. Nevertheless his comment is extraordinarily accurate given the results of the English Church Attendance Survey!

Numbers by age-group

The overall numbers attending church on Sunday by age are given in Table 25, together with a comparison of the English population in the same age-groups:

Table 25: Sunday attendance by age-group, 1998

Age group	Under 15	15–19	20–29	30–44	45–64	65+	TOTAL
Number	717,100	210,600	326,600	646,700	885,800	927,900	3,714,700
% of churchgoers	19	6	9	17	24	25	100%
% of population	19	6	13	23	23	16	100%

It may immediately be seen that the church has many more older people (65 or over) than exist proportionately in the population as a whole. On the other hand there are far fewer young adults (20 to 44).

If these proportions were expressed to give the average age of a churchgoer it would come out at 43^2, compared with 38 in the population. In 1989 both figures were 38, and in 1979 37, as shown in Figure 14. In both 1979 and 1989 there were proportionately more older people in church than in the population, but there were also more younger people to compensate. This lack of younger people in 1998 is what makes the scary title of this chapter seem appropriate.

Figure 14: Average age of churchgoers and population, 1979-1998

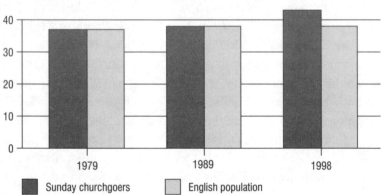

Table 26 repeats the information in the first two lines of Table 25, but in addition gives the same information for 1979 and 1989 for comparison.

Table 26: Sunday attendance by age-group, 1979-1998

Age group	Under 15	15–19	20–29	30–44	45–64	65+	TOTAL
1979	1,416,000	489,700	598,200	870,300	1,087,800	979,000	5,441,000
1989	1,177,000	337,300	481,200	809,400	1,042,500	895,400	4,742,800
1998	717,100	210,600	326,600	646,700	885,800	927,900	3,714,700
% 1979	26	9	11	16	20	18	100%
% 1989	25	7	10	17	22	19	100%
% 1998	19	6	9	17	24	25	100%

This Table shows that in the last two decades of the 20th century:

- The number of young people up to 19 in church has halved.
- The church has also seen a considerable drop in the number attending in their 20s, although these have not quite halved (down 45%).
- Those in their 30s and 40s dropped in the 1980s (by 7%), but dropped three times as much, by 20%, in the 1990s.
- Those aged 45 to 64 have declined, by 4% in the 1980s and by almost 4 times as much, 15%, in the 1990s.
- Those 65 or over dropped 9% in the 1980s, but have recovered in the 1990s, adding 4% to their number, though this did not return them to their 1979 strength.

Figure 15: Numbers going to church on Sunday, 1979-1998

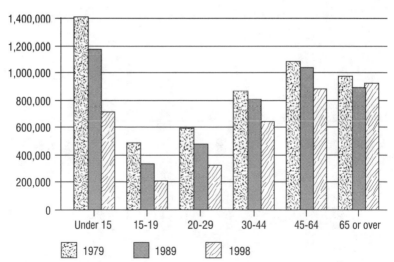

We have therefore a very serious situation – the flight of our youth, the increasing decline of those in "working age", albeit set off slightly by a return of those of grandparent age. The numbers in Table 26 are shown in Figure 15, and the percentages in Figure 16. Figure 17 gives the population proportions.

Figure 16: Percentage of churchgoers by age-group, 1979-1998

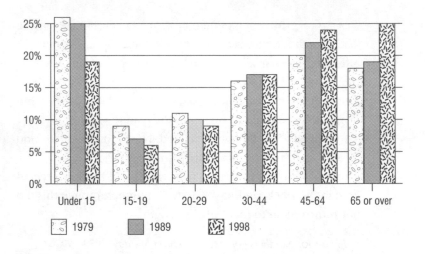

Figure 17: Percentage of population by age-group, 1979-1998

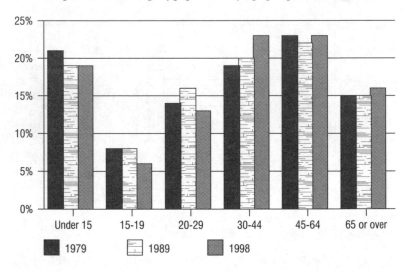

A comparison of Figures 16 and 17 indicates that the drop in those under 15 in the church is much more than might be expected by general population changes. The declines in older teens and those in their 20s is more in line with population movements. The church is missing out in the 1990s in those of parental age with young children (30 to 44), but is doing better than might have been anticipated amongst those aged 45 or over, and especially those aged 65 or over.

These numbers are all church related. They do not include young people going to Christian events or who are part of Christian organisations. Crusaders, for example, had 24,000 members in 1996, Boys' Brigade and Girls' Brigade 166,000[3]. In 1996 such young people totalled 300,000; if half of these only went to a specifically Christian meeting outside the church that would add a sixth on to the numbers of young people connected to Christianity.

Numbers by year

The numbers in Table 26 are large, and whilst their overall nature can be readily discerned, it may be helpful to break down the changes into more "bite-size" chunks. Table 27 therefore takes the numbers in Table 26 and expresses them as a decline per period and the equivalent per week.

Table 27: Net change in the number of Sunday churchgoers by age-group, 1979-1998

Age-group	Total change		Equivalent per week	
	1979–1989	1989–1998	1979–1989	1989–1998
Under 15	–239,000	–459,900	–460	–980
15 to 19	–152,400	–126,700	–290	–270
20 to 29	–117,000	–154,600	–230	–330
30 to 44	– 60,900	–162,700	–120	–350
45 to 64	– 45,300	–156,700	– 90	–340
65 or over	– 83,600	+ 32,500	–160	+70
TOTAL	**–698,200**	**–1,028,100**	**–1,350**	**–2,200**

We were losing 500 children under 15 in the 1980s, that has now doubled to a net outturn of 1,000 boys and girls every week. We were losing 300 teenagers every week in the 1980s, a feature of the previous survey which Youth for Christ and other youth organisations took up with a concerted effort, including the Reaching and Keeping Teenagers study[4]. As a result they have managed to retain more teenagers in the 1990s – the 15 to 19 age-group is the only one (apart from 65 or over) where the loss is less in the 1990s than it was in the 1980s.

We are losing half as many again young men and women in their 20s now than was the case a decade ago, three times as many aged 30 to 44, and 4 times as many in their late 40s and 50s. Many of these will be parents. The only age-group where the tide has turned is in the older group; the churches in England have seen an increase in the numbers of older people coming to church in the 1990s, and this in an age-group naturally hit by higher death rates.

What of the future?

If the trends in Table 26 are projected to 2016, without allowing any alteration in the rate of change, what do we get? The answers are shown in Table 28.

Table 28: Sunday attendance by age-group, 1998-2016

Age group	Under 15	15–19	20–29	30–44	45–64	65+	TOTAL
1998	717,100	210,600	326,600	646,700	885,800	927,900	3,714,700
2016	225,000	85,000	122,000	356,000	617,000	755,000	2,160,000
% 1998	19	6	9	17	24	25	100%
% 2016	10	4	6	16	29	35	100%

I sincerely hope the figures in Table 28 are wrong! The total suggests that 4% of the population may still be attending church on a Sunday (better than the 1% in Chapter 2), but two-thirds, 64%, of these will be 45 years old or over. Almost half the churchgoers, 46%, were under 30 in 1979. If Table 28 is fulfilled that percentage will be 20%. Apart from a revival it is difficult to see how the church can reverse such a steep downward trend. We are one generation from extinction!

With this sombre potential scenario we need to look at what percentage of people are already going to church in different age-groups. This is given in Figure 18.

Figure 18: Percentage of the population in church by age-group, 1979-2016

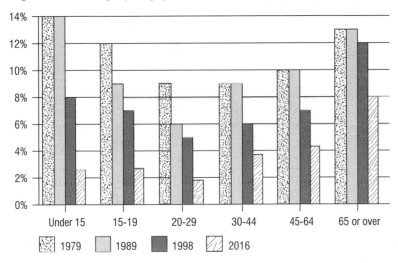

The trends in the current churchgoing numbers are frightening for those who care about the church and the Gospel of Jesus Christ for which it stands. They suggest an indifference, a lack of understanding, commitment and interest perhaps unparalleled since St Augustine came to these shores in 597 AD.

The impact of such decline, if it continues, will be felt not just throughout the churches but throughout all the manifestations of church life, and not least amongst the 6,000 Christian organisations currently listed in the *UK Christian Handbook*[5], many of which will presumably cease to exist. One might also assume that giving to even the large and more established organisations will reduce substantially. With so many elderly people, pro rata, a key emphasis is likely to be on money bequeathed to organisations.

Decadal change

The discussion thus far has been based on the figures for the six age-groups which have been used since the first English Church Census in 1979. It is possible to take these figures, however, and estimate from them the breakdown for every ten years, applying the spread of years in the population to the intermediate church figures. On that basis, we then get the following Table:

Table 29: Numbers attending church by ten year cohorts 1979 to 1998

Age group	1979	1989	1998	Change (1998-1999)
0 to 9	940,000	780,000	480,000	–
10 to 19	960,000	730,000	450,000	–42%
20 to 29	600,000	480,000	330,000	–55%
30 to 39	580,000	540,000	430,000	–10%
40 to 49	560,000	530,000	440,000	–19%
50 to 59	550,000	520,000	430,000	–19%
60 to 69	600,000	510,000	470,000	–10%
70 to 79	430,000	400,000	410,000	–20%
80 or over	220,000	250,000	270,000	–32%
TOTAL	**5,440,000**	**4,740,000**	**3,710,000**	**–22%**

Because 1989 and 1979 are exactly 10 years apart and 1998 and 1989 almost 10 years apart, this Table allows us to trace the various cohorts through the years. Thus of the 940,000 children under 10 in church in 1979, only 730,000 remained ten years later; 210,000 had left. These are net figures, and in reality more than these 210,000 will have left but others in this age-group will have joined instead, and these gross figures are not known. Of the 730,000 aged 10 to 19 in 1989, only 330,000 remained by 1998; 55% had left the church. This percentage is the one given in the last column of the Table; it comes from a diagonal calculation[6].

The final columns in Table 29 show:

- The church has been relatively successful in keeping those attending church on Sunday who were in their 20s in 1989 during the 1990s, as they moved into their 30s.

- It has also kept most of those in their 50s in the 1980s as they moved into their 60s, and retirement age, in the 1990s.

- The church has lost children and teenagers in large numbers on Sundays.

- Sunday attendance amongst those in their 30s and 40s in 1989 has decreased much more than a decade earlier as these people moved into their 40s and 50s. This is the age-group of many parents with younger children, and part of the youth loss will be related to this parental decline.

- The loss of those in their 60s and 70s in 1989 as they moved into their 70s and 80s in the 1990s can be attributed to natural causes! The percentage of people aged 65 and 75 in 1989 who might be expected to die in the next 10 years is respectively 29% and 58%[7]. The fact that the actual loss of churchgoers is so much less either means that churchgoers live longer than non-churchgoers (which could well be true since many neither smoke nor drink alcohol excessively[8]) or that there has been a substantial influx of older people into the churches in the 1990s (which could also well be true with many churches involved with luncheon clubs for the elderly, etc.)

The figures in Table 29 are shown in Figure 19 by age cohort, so that each age-group can as it were be traced across the two decades.

Figure 19: Numbers attending church by cohort, 1979-1998

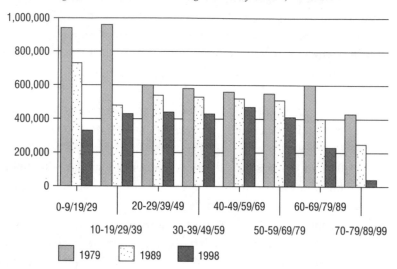

In the 1970s and earlier, before this Figure begins, the churches lost those in their 20s; in the 1980s they lost the teenagers; in the 1990s they lost the children. The age-group which has stayed in church the most consistently in the last 20 years are those who were in their 40s in 1979, and will be in their 60s in 1998. Those younger have dropped out; those older have died off! Those who were in their 40s in 1979 were those born in the 1930s, before the Second World War.

Boomers and Busters

"Boomers" and "Busters" are talked about as if we all know what these terms mean, and as if we all carried in our heads their demographic profile. The Americans had their population boom (where the word "boomers" comes from) in the late 1940s and 1950s, whereas we had ours about 10 years later, largely because of the huge number of Irish immigrants in the late 1950s. But the American way of defining the age-groups allows us to use their categorisations and the years to which they relate without having to alter them. Strictly speaking we should include 1965 in the British "boomers" since that year there was a peak in the number of births, that is, it was the height of the British baby boom.

Seniors *(aged 74 or older in 2000)*

Born in 1926 or earlier these people very likely went to Sunday School as over half the children born in the first part of the 20th century did[9]. No wonder so many of them watch *Songs of Praise* now![10] Many joined the church, and helped church membership reach its peak in 1930 of over 10 million members, 29% of the adult population[11]. They also sent their children to Sunday School even if they stopped going to church themselves.

Builders *(aged 55 to 73 in 2000)*

Born before the end of the Second World War, they are so called because they helped to rebuild the world when the War finished, establishing the economic and social systems we use today. They are the parents of the ...

Boomers *(aged 36 to 54 in 2000)*

These are marginally the largest 'generation' in the UK population. Terry Green, chief executive of Debenhams, explained what they meant to him in an interview, "they have seen the 70s and what that brought: the three-day week and the misery. They have seen the boom of the 80s. Now in the 90s they have been through recession, seen what that involves, and they are a lot wiser. They are not stupid; they have a sensitivity that is not readily understood by many people ..."[12] Of course, the older generations have lived through the 70s and 80s too; the boomers are not uniquely experienced or sensitive, but they have had to carry responsibilities for three generations – their own, their children, and their dependent parents.

The American author Wade Clark Roof has identified four patterns amongst the boomers[13]:

- A diversity of spirituality, reflecting both a consumer culture (searching to find "what works for me"), and a rich and empowering melding of diverse traditions with an emphasis on the relatedness of all things (hence Celtic spirituality, holistic healing, etc),
- A valuing of religious pluralism, with an emphasis on tolerance and respect for others,
- Multilayered belief and practice (such as interest in icons, meditation, spiritual direction, use of candles, and diversity of belief such as churchgoers accepting reincarnation), and
- "Transformed selves", finding personal enhancement in self giving not as the old "giving without counting the cost" but giving /serving both for the sake of others and of self ("how does this help me grow").

All these strands may be found amongst English church people in the 1990s.

Busters *(aged 17 to 35 in 2000)*
A lively article[14] summarised a Commencement Address given by Australian Rowland Croucher at the University of Queensland in March 1998. He described Busters (those who broke through, or "bust", the boom), or Generation Xers, as:

- Survivors of the most aborted generation in history.
- They are also the best educated, most travelled and longest-living generation ever.
- The first to grow up with AIDS, MTV and environmental catastrophes.
- The first electronic generation, having already mastered laptops, the Internet, CD-Roms, faxes, modems, Nintendo, Sega and Play Station. They have a tremendous ability to process lots of information at once. Playing video games while talking on the phone, listening to the radio, doing their home-

work and making a snack was an after school ritual for this generation. This "parallel thinking" allows "multiple task-ing".

- The first generation to be raised completely by TV (so "everything is image") and their musical lyrics are often pas-sionate and angry, sometimes rebellious, mostly honest, sometimes spiritual/religious. There's a pervasive longing for reality, healing, community and peace. One GenXer said, "Music is our lifeblood – I'd rather buy music than eat." And they would rather be at a U2 concert than in church singing hymns.
- Anti-materialistic. So they'll have a succession of jobs, rather than a career. And they'll put relationships before work – work is what you do so that you can have a life.
- Having insatiable appetites for junk food, junk films, junk ideas and junk culture.
- Rejecting institutions. This is a collaborative generation – hierarchies are "out".
- Needing the church more than any other generation and wanting it so little. Although they are "spiritual", they know less about the Bible than any previous generation in the past 1000 years.
- The first "latch-key" generation, with many of them coming from two-job families.
- Affirming diversity and being able to live with ambiguity.
- Fewer than half of them have lived with two biological par-ents throughout their childhood.
- The first generation to grow up without absolute truths, believing that the highest virtue is tolerance of the views of others – post-Christian and post-modern.

Lowell Sheppard, former national director of Youth For Christ in the UK, but now living in Japan, says a "new church is required to reach the new young. It will emphasise the following:

- Creativity and encouragement of individual expression
- Relevant and applied teaching of Scripture
- Affirmation and encouragement of spiritual experiences and demonstrations of supernatural power
- Involvement in holistic mission
- Small and large groups to whom the new young can belong."[15]

The Mosaics *(under 17 in 2000)*
Mosaics gather together fragments of ideas to create their own unique patterns of thinking, in the same way that a patchwork quilt or a Roman mosaic creates a pattern using fragments of material or tile.

How far will the Mosaics fit into the above pattern for Busters? How far will Buster type of thinking make children more or less receptive to the Biblical story? Many such questions can be asked.

Such questions are relevant if the differences, especially the conceptual differences in the way the different generations learn, is noted. For example builders, boosters and boomers were largely trained to think in a linear, logical way.

The age of their teachers is important because their attitude to teaching will vary, and their thinking will be different from the young people. The difference may be seen perhaps in the teaching of history. Builders were taught history, especially English history, across centuries. The school I went to in the 1950s covered 1066 to 1914. This is not how history is taught today. Certain people or periods may be focused on, such as Cromwell, or the Victorian era. The concerns, or principles, of the period would be established. Thus trend thinking is less frequent, and the picture of history is built up as a jigsaw rather than a continuous story. Churchill's *History of the English Speaking Peoples* is not a textbook title today. A number of books have been written exploring these changes in a Christian context[16].

Another element in the generational variations is the importance of relationship between grandparents and grandchildren. One study showed that the family which prays together really does stay together, with churchgoing grandparents more likely to be close to their grandchildren than non-churchgoers[17]. However, another found that children had 10% less contact with grandparents in 1998 than they did in 1988[18]. Increased geographical distance is partly to blame, but this is not the whole reason; there was also less contact by telephone.

Mosaic thinking is not limited to younger people. Glen Hoddle, the former English football coach, is an example. The press said he was a born-again Christian, who consulted his faith healer once a month, and believed in re-incarnation. Patrick Buchanan who ran for USA President in the 1990s was pro-gun, anti-abortion, pro-workers' rights and with a Christian moralist label – both left- and right-wing. He was a sign of the future – a man driven by a cluster of controversial issues which make perfect sense one by one to him and to others.[19]

Generational variations

Table 30 summarises the above categories[20], and introduces thereby the latest one. A sixth has been added, the Kaleidoscopes (my title), deliberately thereby suggesting that the next generation will not look at one static picture as in a Roman mosaic, but rather a moving mix of pictures, all made of the same parts. Just as the Mosaics have been called Generation Y, as the children of generation X, so it is likely that this generation will be called Generation Z. We cannot ignore this generation, and need to start preparing for it now in the church.

Table 30: Six Generations of British People

Generation	Years of birth	Age range in 2000	Estimated UK population in 2001
Seniors	1926 and earlier	74 +	4.5 million
Builders[1]	1927-45	55 to 73	12.4 million
Boomers	1946-64	36 to 54	15.1 million
Busters[2]	1965-83	17 to 35	14.6 million
Mosaics[3]	1984-02	Up to 16	12.6 million
Kaleidoscopes	2003-21	To be born!	0 million

1 Also called Boosters or the Maturity Generation in some literature
2 Also called Generation X or Friends in some literature
3 Also called Beepers (because they have grown up in the IT age), the Millennium Generation, Generation Y, or Thatcher's Children in some literature, especially British

As the church grapples with the demise of youth in its midst, it needs to learn some of the differences between these generations. For example,

- Builders respect status; boomers respect competence; busters respect openness
- Builders can manage without support; boomers like support; busters need support
- Builders are happy to do any job; boomers are more specialist; busters look at the team doing the building first
- Builders attend church out of habit; boomers like to use their gifts; busters attend when they feel like it
- Seniors, builders and boomers think linearly and logically in the main; busters think creatively; mosaics focus on parts of the picture[21].

Leaving church having tried Sunday School

A 1993 study, *Reaching and Keeping Teenagers*[22], found that on average children stayed in Sunday School about 4 years before they left, if they were going to leave. The Sunday School lesson has to be relevant, the lack of which may have caused teenagers to say it was "boring" rather than the more sophisticated evaluation "irrelevant". Rev Dr Alister McGrath, principal of Wycliffe Hall, an Anglican theological college, says "Above all, we need to take the trouble to relate the message to its audience, making sure that it scratches where people itch."[23] The difficulty of poor Sunday Schools is that there is now a generation who have had some church experience who are currently outside the church, and don't wish to return. "We've tried it already," they say.

As mentioned in the last Chapter, why people leave church is the subject of the book *Gone but not Forgotten*.[24] Philip Richter and Leslie Francis analysed the material by whether the respondents were over or under 20, and there was one area where there was a major difference. This is what the authors call "stage of faith" and is a reference to the work on faith development[25] by Professor James Fowler of the Center for Research in Faith and Moral Development at Emory University in Atlanta, Georgia, United States. He diagnosed 6 stages of faith and analysed these by age-group, using titles adapted from another book[26]:

- 1: Impressionistic faith (early childhood)
- 2: Ordering faith (childhood or beyond)
- 3: Conforming faith (adolescence and beyond)
- 4: Choosing faith (young adulthood and beyond)
- 5: Balanced faith (early mid-life and beyond)
- 6: Selfless faith (mid-life and beyond)

If people are leaving before the age of 20 for Faith-stage reasons this suggests that they do so as they begin to move from Stage 3 to Stage 4 as the majority of teenagers are in Stage 3 and those in their 20s in Stage 4. It could simply be the cost of discipleship, or a realisation of the implications of what the Christian life involves, that causes some to leave. This parallels the findings of a survey by Dr Eddie Gibbs, Professor of Church Growth at Fuller Theological Seminary, California, of why people leave[27].

Sunday School teaching

Fewer people wish to teach in Sunday School today particularly on a regular, committed basis. They may attend church less frequently than weekly and wish to be part of the main service rather than teach when they do come. They may not know how to teach in today's teaching culture, or how to control noisy children. Some do not know their Christian faith well enough to be able to answer children's questions. Those who do teach often want to stop being a teacher after a relatively short time. Many teachers now teach on a rota system, so are actually with the children less frequently. This means more teachers are needed, but these are being selected from a decreasing pool of people as those aged 30 to 44 and 45 to 64 are leaving the church. So more demands are made of those who remain. This can cause more to leave, or those who are actually poor at teaching to be in the position of teacher.

Children also appear less regularly. This means that Sunday School preparation is difficult. One teacher had 6 children one week and 25 the next. Children are not always brought by parents, but sometimes by grandparents or neighbours, so getting to know the family is less straightforward. Infrequent attendance also means that the children don't necessarily get to know the other children very well.

Lessons are less easy to prepare. The way children are taught today is different from the way that many of the teachers themselves were taught. Children learn differently – mosaics take in information at a faster rate than boomers or builders (who are the majority of Sunday School teachers). Mosaics tune out after 6 to 8 minutes unless a transition catches their interest. They have far far less Bible background knowledge so need to be given much more detail. The words being used to teach must be less theological, judgmental, or paternalistic. There is the constant need to use more technology, if only because children very often attribute greater truth to a technological source of information than they do a person[28], and also because they are steeped in technology at home and at day school.

Teaching materials have to change with the times. In some churches, individual teachers choose what teaching material they wish to use. This sometimes means that more than one type is used within the same Sunday School!

And whatever teaching notes are used, some wish to change it every so often just because they want to change! Some Sunday Schools wish to have Lectionary based materials; others don't. Teaching materials need to include information on how to teach the Bible as well as what to teach from the Bible. Teaching materials may not assume that other Christian related activities, like Bible-reading, will necessarily be used. Only 49% of churches encourage children to read the Bible.[29]

Competition with the Sunday School

There are also now more alternative activities available on Sundays than previously such as sporting events, musical festivals and shopping. Many families, even Christian ones, think of Sundays firstly as visiting days and for split families, Sunday can be "Daddy's day".

As a consequence, some churches are moving Sunday School to a weeknight, where it becomes "Wednesday School" or whatever. However, it can then compete with other youth activities run by the church or others, including uniformed organisations. Conversely, uniformed organisations and other youth activities may transfer their work to a Sunday in order to attract larger numbers. This also means a possible conflict with Sunday School.

Behind such changes are the issues of priorities, and behind priorities lies overall church strategy. But many churches don't have a youth strategy (or any other!). How can the ministers and leaders be helped to shape a strategic plan for their church for the next, say, 5 years?

It is clear that the methods and techniques for children's work have changed drastically, and the children themselves have changed also. And the changing process is continuing. Sunday School has an honourable history, but the institution needs renewal, as it is still vital to reach young people with the Gospel from the earliest age possible. This is still the most responsive period of their lives[30].

Unless churches can face the challenge of thinking differently and acting strategically, taking risks in the process, it may well be that George Carey's words get unintended fulfilment – one generation to extinction.

Young people

What does this mean for commitment? Only 14% of girls and 22% of boys agree that "where there are children in the family, parents should stay together even if they don't get along."[31] If commitment to the most intimate union known to human beings is repeatedly thrown asunder, what of other commitments?

On a much lesser scale, commitment to church membership has declined, as it has with membership to many other organisations, a characteristic of today's society. What then of commitment to even deeper things than organisations or people to Christ? Will there be a tendency for those who are Christians in their 20s today, for example, to say in their 40s, "Well, I've followed Christianity for the last 20 years, now I'll try Buddhism."?

The Biblical basis of commitment, or perseverance, is very strong. "The one who endures to the end will be saved"[32] is but one text of many. In our dealings with young people today, how do we help encourage their commitment to spiritual values and beliefs? Commitment is partly built up around action. Do we need to teach again the importance of a daily act of devotion? To express one's faith in specific behaviours? Commitment is also partly based on one's appreciation of the value of another person, or object, or organisation. It also reflects one's own integrity.

This issue was highlighted by evidence given to the Parliamentary Hearing on the Family in the United Nations Year of the Family in 1994. Dr Kiernan, senior research fellow in demography at the London School of Economics, in presenting her case said that the main engine driving the change in couples living together is that of partnership behaviour. Partnerships were not relationships, and were of a different quality. Marriage is now seen as such an alliance, a relationship, not a partnership. Hence the need to teach about relationships in terms of acceptance, tolerance, expectations and communications. Cohabitation is another form of relationship, not a partnership. A partnership often begins when a couple have a baby, or at least, is perceived as needing to begin: 70% in 1989 accepted the statement "people who want children ought to get married"[33].

The Cambridge-based Relationships Foundation started by Dr Michael Schluter has identified a further category of those who are disadvantaged: "the relationally deprived"[34]. Nigel Lee, head of student ministries at the Universities and Colleges Christian Fellowship, told a meeting at which I was present[35] of how there is "less and less communal space in new student accommodation". There was a diminution of mature social conversation. The consequence was a lack of understanding of relationships with anybody (let alone Jesus Christ), and hence a need for teaching on this topic.

This becomes especially important when teenagers want to talk things over with their parents. Fitting in these times of precious conversation (invariably at the most inconvenient and pressurised times of the day!) becomes a priority. Andy Hickford, former youth pastor in Luton, said, "we soon discovered that a teenager's world revolved around school and family"[36]. Another church leader said, "the problems of growing up in a divorced or remarried home makes teenagers more realistic of the need of something beyond themselves to help themselves, especially women."

Parents

Much has and is being written about young people; less is written about the problems that many parents, let alone Christian parents, face. Demographically, boomers, those aged 36 to 54, are the majority generation. They are a key component of people in employment, who increase in numbers up till 2011, but then decline as they retire.

Women have entered the working population in large numbers. The size of families has also fallen – from an average of 2.45 children in the 1930s to an estimated 1.80 for women born after 1975, 14% less than the 2.1 required to replace the population (immigration apart) if mortality rates were constant. The proportion of women who will never have a child is rising (from 1 in 10 to perhaps 1 in 4); they are also starting their families later, obviously another contributing factor to smaller families, mainly because they are marrying later, having spent time seeking to find fulfilment in a career and/or establishing a certain level of material prosperity.

The proportions of single parents or unmarried parents who are in church are smaller than population proportions in every survey where this has been measured. It is partly because churches often do not welcome those whose lifestyle is judged inappropriate or just plain wrong. So about a third of children in the country who live with such parents are unlikely even to be considered for Sunday School, again making the numbers attending sharply down.

If there are fewer parents in general, then there will be fewer parents in church, and if parents are the most likely to be willing to be Sunday School teachers (because they have first hand experience of children) then the numbers of potential teachers will continue to fall. Of course there are many single or childless married women who also help in Sunday School, but will they continue to come forward in such numbers as they have done?

Present trends also mean that parents are older today than they were   and therefore possibly have less energy. If both partners are working, they do not necessarily want to have commitments such as going to church on their day off.

It is possible that the Christian divorce and remarriage rate is about half that of the national divorce rate[37]. Even so, that still means that many Christians are in divorced or remarried families. Nationally 9% of men and 6% of women are in their second or third marriage. Many of these 2 million households include children and step-children. In many, the parents will often assume that their marital experience makes them unsuitable for participation in church, and the children/step-children in their household again are less likely to attend Sunday School. Hence a further reduction in overall numbers, both of children and parents.

Older people

On the other hand, as the above figures make clear, older people are joining or re-joining the churches in good numbers. Why should this be? Perhaps because of the emphasis on adult evangelism that has strongly emerged in the 1980s and 1990s, courses like Alpha or

Emmaus which are primarily designed for adults, or the emergence of organisations like Outlook especially concerned for reaching elderly people. Others, like the Methodist Homes for the Aged, have also moved from only concentrating on accommodation to thinking through the needs of older churchgoers, and publishing books and other material to help churches with the issues. In addition, as people near the end of their lives and face such factors as increasing lack of physical mobility, illness, passing on of friends, loneliness and so on, they feel a personal faith is more relevant to their needs.

One of the most successful regular BBC programmes, which will celebrate its 40th anniversary early in the 3rd millennium, is *Songs of Praise.* Figure 20 compares the ages of those watching it in 1998 with those attending church.

Figure 20: Millions watching Songs of Praise *and attending church by age, 1998*

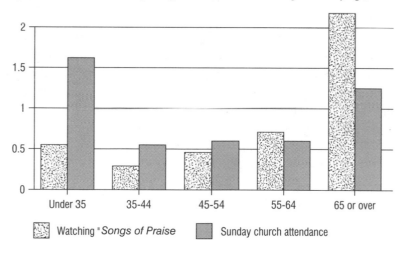

This compares the 2.2 million people 65 or over who watch *Songs of Praise* each week, averaged over the whole year, with the 1.25 million people in church[38]. It indicates that there are about a million people watching *Songs of Praise* who don't go to church, and since it is unlikely that all the churchgoers 65 or over will watch the BBC programme, the number of non-churchgoers watching it is almost certainly in excess of a million. Add in those aged 55 to 64 who are in excess of the church numbers, and it means that 1.9% of the population are watching *Songs of Praise* who do not attend church.

Figure 21 shows the social class of those watching the programme. Since the majority are C2 or DE, the group that used to be called "working class" and which has tended to be poorly represented in the church in most studies of the social class of churchgoers, this suggests that whilst the churches may not be providing spiritual input for older people, or working class folk, *Songs of Praise* is!

Figure 21: Social class of those watching Songs of Praise and the population, 1998

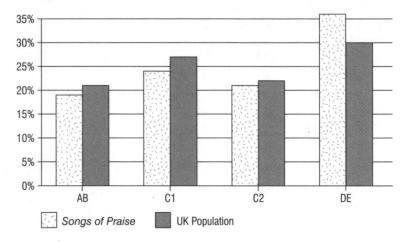

Older people are important for the church in terms of commitment, faithfulness and prayerfulness even if less so in financial terms, and they often have a realistic view of the minister, who frequently will be about the same age as their children. They will therefore tend to treat them as such!

Table 31: Age distribution of English churchgoers by Denomination

Category	Year	<15 %	15–19 %	20–29 %	30–44 %	45–64 %	65+ %	Total(=100%)	Avg*
TOTAL of all	**1979**	*26*	*9*	*11*	*16*	*20*	*18*	**5,441,000**	**37**
English	**1989**	*25*	*7*	*10*	*17*	*22*	*19*	**4,742,800**	**38**
Churchgoers	**1998**	*19*	*6*	*9*	*17*	*24*	*25*	**3,714,700**	**43**
Anglicans	1979	27	9	10	17	18	19	1,671,000	36
	1989	24	5	8	17	24	22	1,491,900	41
	1998	18	4	7	16	26	29	980,600	46
Baptists	1979	30	8	9	16	19	18	290,000	36
	1989	26	7	10	18	20	19	270,900	37
	1998	22	6	9	18	22	23	277,600	41
Catholics	1979	24	12	12	19	20	13	1,991,000	35
	1989	24	8	11	18	23	16	1,715,900	37
	1998	18	6	10	19	25	22	1,230,100	42
Independent and	1979	31	9	13	17	14	16	299,000	33
New Churches	1989	31	16	13	18	13	9	425,500	29
	1998	23	7	12	21	20	17	392,100	37
of which: Independent	1998	19	5	8	16	23	28	161,600	44
New Churches	1998	26	9	15	25	18	7	230,500	32
Methodist	1979	28	5	5	12	25	25	621,000	41
	1989	23	5	7	12	23	30	512,300	44
	1998	19	4	4	11	24	38	379,700	49
Orthodox	1979	27	12	6	13	23	19	10,000	37
	1989	24	7	12	14	25	18	12,300	38
	1998	17	12	11	17	20	23	25,200	41
Pentecostal	1979	33	11	12	18	16	10	228,000	30
	1989	31	9	15	18	17	10	236,700	31
	1998	27	8	14	22	19	10	214,600	33
United Reformed	1979	27	5	7	14	21	26	190,000	41
	1989	24	4	6	13	23	30	149,300	44
	1998	18	3	5	12	24	38	121,700	49
Other denominations	1979	25	9	11	16	20	19	141,000	37
	1989	27	6	8	14	21	24	113,600	40
	1998	18	5	9	16	23	29	93,100	45
English Population	**1979**	*21*	*8*	*14*	*19*	*23*	*15*	**46.4mn**	**37**
	1989	*19*	*8*	*16*	*20*	*22*	*15*	**47.7mn**	**38**
	1998	*20*	*6*	*13*	*22*	*23*	*16*	**49.7mn**	**38**

*Taking "65 and over" as having an average age of 75.

Church attendance by age and denomination

On the previous page, Table 31 gives the percentages of Sunday churchgoers by denomination not just for 1998 with the latest figures, but for the previous studies as well[39] for ease of comparison.

The Orthodox, Anglicans, Methodists and the United Reformed have lost the most children in percentage terms, although because the Orthodox have grown overall the actual number of children attending their churches has increased. The Independents have lost the most teenagers, the Anglicans the most in their 20s. The Anglicans have gained the most aged 45 to 64, especially in the 1980s.

The data in this table may be used in at least three ways – it may be compared with:
* The same denomination but previous years
* Other denominations but the same year
* The population of the country.

The following three bar-charts take these respectively with different denominations as examples.

Figure 22: Anglican churchgoers by age, 1979-1998

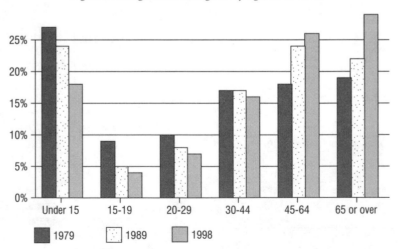

This shows the drop in children in the Anglican church in the 1990s, as the earlier study showed the decline of older teens in the 1980s. The strong growth of those aged 45 to 64 in the 1980s, mainly women, was not repeated in the 1990s, though those aged 65 demonstrate a marked increase in church attendance.

Figure 23: Church attendance in three denominations by age, 1998

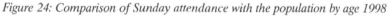

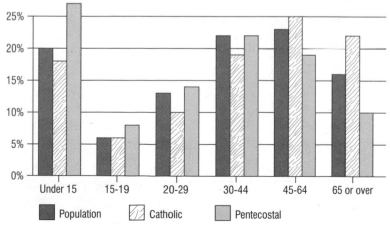

Figure 24: Comparison of Sunday attendance with the population by age 1998

It is obvious that the experience of church for those attending the three denominations in Figure 23 will be very different! Half, 50%, of the New Church attenders are under 30, whereas only a quarter, 27%, of Methodists are. Church programmes as well as Sunday worship will vary to meet the different age-groups present. The worry for the Methodists is how to attract those of younger age.

The Catholics in Figure 24 are closer to the population profile than the Pentecostals, but have fewer children, despite their many schools, and more older people. The Pentecostals have more children but fewer elderly. This is partly because many in the black African churches, who are part of this grouping, retire home to Jamaica where a British pension gives a more comfortable living.

Church attendance by age and churchmanship

Table 32 gives figures similar to Table 31 but for churchmanship. As this was not asked in 1979, figures relate to the latter two years only. The overall figures and population figures are of course the same so are not repeated in this Table.

Table 32 shows that the greatest drop in the proportion of children is among the Evangelicals, and in the latter it is the Mainstream and Charismatics who have seen the greatest fall. The Anglo-Catholics have a large decline in the percentage of older teenagers. There is relatively little change in the percentage of those attending in their 20s.

The percentage of those attending aged 30 to 44 has increased amongst Mainstream and Charismatic Evangelicals and the Catholics. This age-group will usually contain a number of parents with young children who might be expected to come with them to church/Sunday School. As the percentage of children in these two groups has also declined this could suggest that it is the numbers of children coming to their Sunday Schools without their parents (presumably children of non-church families) who have specially decreased.

Table 32: Age distribution of English churchgoers by Churchmanship

| Category | Year | Age-group | | | | | | Total(=100%) | Avg* |
		<15 %	15–19 %	20–29 %	30–44 %	45–64 %	65+ %		
Anglo-Catholic	1989	19	9	8	17	24	23	178,300	42
	1998	17	5	7	15	27	29	177,600	46
Broad	1989	22	5	7	15	25	26	434,000	43
	1998	20	3	6	13	25	33	352,400	47
Catholic	1989	24	9	10	17	23	17	1,867,500	38
	1998	18	7	11	20	24	20	980,000	41
Evangelical: Total	1989	30	7	10	18	18	17	1,430,400	35
	1998	22	6	10	19	22	21	1,391,300	40
Evangelical: Broad	1989	24	6	8	16	22	24	414,600	41
	1998	19	4	6	15	24	32	217,900	46
Evangelical: Mainstream	1989	33	8	9	14	18	18	384,600	35
	1998	21	6	9	18	22	24	645,500	42
Evangelical: Charismatic	1989	32	8	13	20	17	10	631,200	31
	1998	23	8	12	23	20	14	527,900	36
Liberal	1989	22	6	8	15	24	25	479,900	42
	1998	17	4	6	13	26	34	425,500	48
Low Church	1989	23	5	7	14	24	27	280,500	43
	1998	20	4	5	14	24	33	275,400	46
All others	1989	18	6	11	17	23	25	72,200	43
	1998	14	8	9	17	23	29	112,500	45

*Taking "65 and over" as having an average age of 75.

It is the same groups, together with the Anglo-Catholics, who have seen the main increase in the proportions of those coming aged 45 to 64. Could this imply the same reason for the decline in attendance of older children?

It is the Broad, Broad Evangelical and Liberal categories who have seen an increase above the average in the oldest group, 65 or over. All three have the highest average ages. The Liberals have increased the most which explains why the average age of Liberals is the highest in the Table. Only the Charismatics continue to have an average age in the 30s. Figure 25 shows the difference between these two extremes of the distribution, together with the Low Church, and Figure 26 the change amongst the Catholics.

Figure 27 compares all the churchmanship categories in three

broad age-groups for ease of showing the differences between them.
Each pair of columns gives the age-groups for 1989 and 1998.

Figure 25: Church attendance in three churchmanships by age, 1998

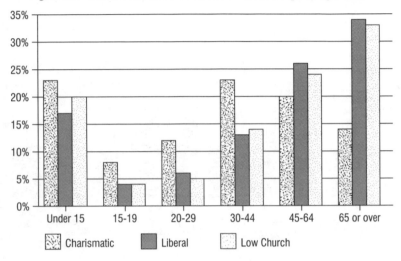

Figure 26: Change amongst Catholic Sunday attendance 1989-1998

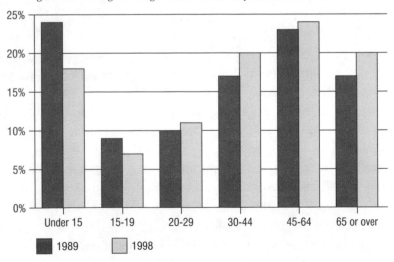

Figure 27: Sunday attendance by churchmanship by age, 1989-1998

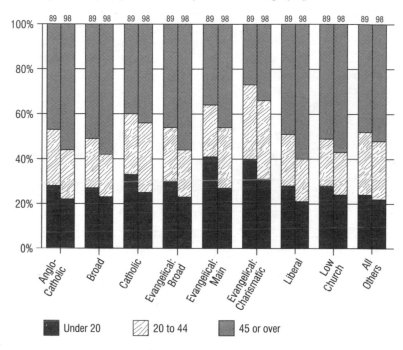

Church attendance by age and region

Table 33 overleaf gives similar information as for denomination and churchmanship, but this time for Region, with a three year comparison possible this time.

The North Region has seen the greatest decline with respect to age, and South East (South) the least. While East Anglia, South East (South) and the South West have the greatest proportions of elderly people in the population, churchgoers in the first and last of these have only changed with the average or overall change, showing that despite more older people in congregations generally these have not come in in sufficient numbers to make the average age higher. In the South East (South) there has been a much smaller decline in the proportions of children 1979 to 1998.

Table 33: Age distribution of English churchgoers by Region

Category	Year	<15 %	15–19 %	20–29 %	30–44 %	45–64 %	65+ %	Total(=100%)	Avg*
TOTAL	**1979**	**26**	**9**	**11**	**16**	**20**	**18**	**5,441,000**	**37**
of all English	**1989**	**25**	**7**	**10**	**17**	**22**	**19**	**4,742,800**	**38**
Churchgoers	**1998**	**19**	**6**	**9**	**17**	**24**	**25**	**3,714,700**	**43**
North	1979	25	9	9	17	23	17	365,300	37
	1989	23	7	10	15	24	21	312,500	40
	1998	16	5	8	16	26	29	225,100	46
Yorks/Humberside	1979	24	9	10	16	21	20	512,200	38
	1989	25	7	9	16	22	21	429,600	39
	1998	19	5	8	17	25	26	286,400	44
North West	1979	27	9	11	16	19	18	960,500	36
	1989	26	7	9	16	23	19	793,100	38
	1998	18	6	8	16	25	27	556,800	44
East Midlands	1979	27	7	9	16	21	20	384,200	38
	1989	26	7	8	16	22	21	328,600	39
	1998	20	5	8	17	23	27	260,800	43
West Midlands	1979	26	9	11	18	21	15	574,800	36
	1989	24	7	9	16	23	21	516,700	39
	1998	20	6	8	17	25	24	363,000	42
East Anglia	1979	25	7	12	16	21	19	250,700	38
	1989	25	7	8	16	22	22	224,400	39
	1998	20	5	8	16	23	28	162,400	44
South East (North)	1979	28	9	11	17	20	15	520,400	35
	1989	27	8	10	18	20	17	445,300	36
	1998	19	6	9	19	24	23	386,900	42
South East	1979	33	8	11	14	18	16	696,000	34
(Greater London)	1989	24	7	12	20	21	16	649,600	37
	1998	21	6	12	20	22	19	617,900	39
South East (South)	1979	23	10	11	17	20	19	615,900	38
	1989	25	8	8	18	21	20	544,100	38
	1998	20	6	9	17	24	24	479,000	42
South West	1979	24	8	9	16	21	22	561,000	39
	1989	24	8	8	15	22	23	498,900	40
	1998	19	5	7	16	23	30	376,400	45
English Population	**1979**	**21**	**8**	**14**	**19**	**23**	**15**	**46.4mn**	**37**
	1989	**19**	**8**	**16**	**20**	**22**	**15**	**47.7mn**	**38**
	1998	**20**	**6**	**13**	**22**	**23**	**16**	**49.7mn**	**38**

*Taking "65 and over" as having an average age of 75.

Other countries

The figures given in this Chapter are fairly grim for those wanting to see the church grow, especially through the next generation. While they reveal a crisis situation in England, Welsh church attendance has fared worse[40], although Scottish attendance has fared better[41], perhaps because the latest figures relate to 1994 and the larger decline seem perhaps to have happened in the later 1990s. The Australian data comes with considerable estimation since the source books do not give the data in the form required; they suggest however similar trends to those found in Britain. Table 34 gives details.

Table 34: Church attendance in Great Britain and Australia, various years

		<15 %	15–19 %	20–29 %	30–44 %	45–64 %	65+ %	Total(=100%)	Avg*
Category	Year								
England	1979	26	9	11	16	20	18	5,441,000	37
	1989	25	7	10	17	22	19	4,742,800	38
	1998	19	6	9	17	24	25	3,714,700	43
Wales	1982	26	7	8	14	22	23	280,100	40
	1995	17	4	7	14	26	32	253,100	47
Scotland	1984	25	5	9	15	24	22	863,000	40
	1994	23	5	8	16	25	23	746,000	42
Australia[42]	1983	22	6	8	14	30	20	3,654,000	41
	1996	20 **	5	7	19	29	20	1,700,100	42

Age-group

*Taking "65 and over" as having an average age of 75.   **This figure is estimated

How do I use this information?

A number of churches already regularly analyse their attendance and/or membership by age, and several enclosed copies of graphs or diagrams showing their different figures. At a 1998 seminar held in Bolton the chair[43] asked, "What are the most important statistics for ministers to watch?" and the answer given was that age is one of them. So this practice of analysing a particular congregation and doing so at regular intervals is to be encouraged. Trend information is also a key indicator to seeing how a ministry is moving. In many cases churches broke down their information by gender, and this is worth doing if possible, although the ECAS study happened not to ask for it.

Here, for example, are two sets of figures sent in, one from a Church of England parish in Derbyshire, and one from a Salvation Army Corps, or church, in South London. The first was 1998, the second 1995. Both were Mainstream Evangelical churches. Their figures are given in Table 35, together with the relevant figures for comparison from previous Tables, the Other denominations figures being used as these include the Salvation Army:

Table 35: Actual results from two congregations

		Age-group							
		<15	15–19	20–29	30–44	45–64	65+		
Church	Year	%	%	%	%	%	%	Total(=100%)	Avg*
Church of England	1998	**20**	**4**	**6**	**18**	**35**	**17**	**135**	**42**
Salvation Army	1995	**13**	**3**	**9**	**9**	**29**	**37**	**156**	**51**
Anglican	1998	18	4	7	16	26	29	980,600	46
Other denominations	1998	18	5	9	16	23	29	93,100	45
Evan: Mainstream	1998	21	6	9	18	22	24	645,500	42
East Midlands	1998	20	5	8	17	23	27	260,800	43
Greater London	1998	21	6	12	20	22	19	617,900	39

The first thing to do is to group your average Sunday church attendance in the 6 age-groups used, and then express your numbers as percentages. You then get the equivalent of the top two rows in Table 35.

Secondly, pull out from the earlier Tables the relevant figures for your denomination, churchmanship and region. You then get the equivalent of the last five rows in Table 35.

Thirdly, compare your figures with each of these. The survey figures are taken from a large sample but even so, as explained in Chapter 1, they will in reality be ±1 or 2%. So small differences between the ECAS results and your figures ignore. Look for large differences.

Fourthly, note where your figures are larger than the ECAS results (your strengths) and where your figures are lower (your weaknesses). Then pause to think, what can we do to build on our strengths – a campaign to attract more like that, extra services, some kind of community service? Then ask, what can we do to begin to overcome our weaknesses? Add to the leadership team, change the way we do things, prepare new publicity?

So, for example, taken the Church of England parish given above. When comparing with the age percentages the church had many more aged 45 to 64, and fewer aged 65 or over. In fact their percentages were so much larger that they dominated whether the comparison was with denomination, churchmanship or region. So the church is strong in those aged 45 to 64. Why is this? Many of these people are likely to be parents of teenage children – do they come because of the church's children's work (unlikely because there aren't many teenagers). Are they older single people? Does the church have House groups? Many of these will attend such. Is this more intimate fellowship attracting people? If so, do they need to publicise a sermon series "Looking for friendship"? Is there a good Men's Fellowship or Women's Group? Does the church seek to encourage people to come because of their gender? In fact the details supplied by this church did give gender information, and two-thirds in this group were women. Does this mean there were married women without their partners? Might "Praying for your unconverted partner" be a topic for discussion? While some in this group may be in a new job, most will be working, and likely to have been in the same workplace for some years. Have a service for people's workmates? You can see the thinking – how do we build on our strength?

The Salvation Army Corps is also strong on those aged 45 to 64, but has other elements of importance. It is low on children, and in those aged 30 to 44, the age when many are parents of young children. This suggests the importance of targeting families. What family activities currently take place? What publicity is there for them? Do children not come because they have other things to do on

Sunday? Change Sunday School, as the Salvation Army in Bromley did, to Monday School? Do parents come with small children, and there's no creche? Start a Mum's and Toddler's Group? Begin a child minding facility after school to keep the children off the streets? Hold a party for all the children in the neighbourhood aged 10 say? Does the leader make a point of going to local schools for RE lessons or Assemblies to get his Corps known more? Does the leader put on parenting classes and advertise these widely? Or show "Focus on the Family" films or lend/hire out relevant Christian videos? How are the existing people in this age-group being used, and what do they suggest? The church is also very strong on elderly people. How best teach these to be mission minded, and share their faith with others of similar age? What does the church need to do to draw more elderly people in – a coffee morning for old-timers? A prescription collection facility (the average person over 65 years of age uses 30 prescriptions a year)? You will notice that whilst this Corps has fewer folk in their 20s, they have greater deficiencies elsewhere, and it is the size of these which can *help determine the priorities of the Corps,* since no church can do everything.

There is also the spiritual dimension. We need to pray more and seek God's face and His power and guidance. Unless churches can grapple with this and the strategic thinking and planning required from an examination of factors like these, we are in danger of truly becoming one generation from extinction.

SUMMARY

1 Sunday church attendance has declined by an average of 2,200 people every week in the 1990s.

2 Half of the overall loss in the 1990s was amongst children under the age of 15. Many children today think mosaically, and the church has to find better ways of relating to them.

3 The greatest percentage loss was amongst teenagers, 10 to 19.

4 There was also a decline in the 1990s, greater than in the 1980s, of those aged 30 to 44, perhaps because more were working.

5 The smallest loss was amongst those in their 50s in the 1980s as they moved into their 60s.

6 There has been a net increase into the church during the 1990s of those aged 65 and over.

7 If present trends continue, we could literally be one generation from extinction.

8 Sunday Schools are decreasing in numbers and many churches are finding it hard to recruit sufficient teachers.

9 There is more competition now on a Sunday; churches face the challenge of thinking differently.

10 Looking at a church's attendance by age-group by denomination, churchmanship or region allows strengths and weaknesses to be identified for strategic thinking and action.

NOTES

1. The Rt Hon and Most Rev Archbishop George Carey, speaking at the Church of England Board of Mission Cofnerence, 9th March 1999, and reported in the *Daily Telegraph*, 10th March.
2. Taking those 65 or over as 75 years of age.
3. Brierley, Dr Peter, editor, *Religious Trends*, No 1, 1999/2000, 1998, Paternoster Publishing, Carlisle and Christian research, London, Table 4.10.1.
4. Brierley, Dr Peter, *Reaching and Keeping Teenagers*, 1993, Monarch Publications, Crowborough, East Sussex.
5. Wraight, Heather and Brierley, Dr Peter, editors, *UK Christian Handbook*, 2000/2001 edition, 1999, HarperCollins and Christian Research, London.
6. The figure obtained is $330,000 \div 730,000 = 0.45$. This, as a percentage is 45%, which taken from 100 is 55%, the figure given. Other percentages in this column are calculated likewise.
7. *English Life Tables*, No 15, 1990-1992, Government Actuary's Department, 1998.
8. See, for example, the evidence from American Seventh-Day Adventists given in Brierley, Peter, editor, *Act on the Facts*, 1992, MARC Europe, London, Page 165.
9. 56% of the child population were in Sunday School in 1905, a percentage which dropped only very slowly for the next 20 years. The detailed figures are in Table 2.15, Brierley, Dr Peter, editor, *Religious Trends*, No 2, 2000/2001, 1999, Christian Research and HarperCollins, London.
10. Ibid., Figure 6.5.5.
11. Ibid., Table 8.17.
12. Article *"The Davidson interview: Terry Green"* by Andrew Davidson, in *Management Today*, Corby, January 1999, Page 40
13. Roof, Wade Clark, *A Generation of Seekers: The Spiritual Journeys of the Baby Boom Generation*, 1994, HarperCollins, San Francisco, and reported in *ReSearch*, Bulletin No 15 of the Christian Research Association, New Zealand, Summer Issue 1997, Page 3.
14. Article *"The Truth is Out There!"* by Rev Dr Rowland Croucher, in *Ministry Today*, Issue 14, October 1998, Page 27.
15. Summary of dissertation *"Mission to the New Young of Japan"*, sent by e-mail 26th November 1998, and available from kandesan@gol.com.
16. For example, *Jesus for a New Generation* by Kevin Ford; or *Generationext*, George Barna, Regal, Ventura, California, 1995.

17. *Daily Telegraph* report, 24th August 1998, based on study of 500 American families in Iowa, studied by Dr Valarie King, Penn State University.
18. *Guardian* report, 5th May 1998, on a Family Policy Studies Centre survey, mentioned in the R Briefing, Issue 20, August 1998.
19. Example taken from Dixon, Dr Patrick, *Futurewise,* 1998, HarperCollins, London, Page 240.
20. Based on Barna, George, 1998, *The Second Coming of the Church,* Word Publishing, London, Page 72.
21. Based on Taylor, Dr William, editor, 1997, *Too Valuable to Lose,* William Carey Library, Pasadena, California, United States, Page 48, but taken from *12 Things to Wake Up To!,* Brierley, Dr Peter, 1999, Christian Research, London, Page 7.
22. Op cit (Item 4).
23. McGrath, Rev Alister and Green, Rev Michael, 1994, *Springboard for Faith,* Hodder & Stoughton, London, Page 53, and quoted in *Understanding the Times,* Church of Scotland, St Andrew Press, 1995, Page 34.
24. Richter, Philip and Francis, Professor Leslie, 1998, *Gone but not Forgotten,* Darton, Longman and Todd, London, Page 137.
25. A summary of this may be found in op cit (Item 4), Pages 158-160.
26. Astley, Dr Jeff, 1992, *How Faith Grows, Faith Development and Christian Education,* National Society/Church House Publishing, London.
27. Gibbs, Professor Eddie, 1993, *Winning Them Back,* Monarch, Crowborough, East Sussex, Table 9, Page 278.
28. Barna, George, 1998, *The Second Coming of the Church,* Word Publishing, London, Page 58.
29. Private research for a youth organisation by Christian Research, London, December 1998.
30. This is taken further in Brierley, Dr Peter, *Steps to the Future,* 2000, Christian Research, London and Scripture Union, Bletchley.
31. Article *"Family Matters"* by Dr Clifford Hill, Prophecy Today, Volume 14 Number 4, July/August 1998, Page 11.
32. Matthew chapter 24 verse 13.
33. Kiernan, Kathleen E, and Estaugh, Valerie, 1993, *Cohabitation, Extra-marital childbearing and social policy*, by Family Policy Studies Centre, London, Occasional Paper No 17, Page 7.
34. Mass circulated letter from The R Foundation, Cambridge, by Dr Michael Schluter, July 1998.
35. Council Meeting of the Evangelical Missionary Alliance held on 26th January 1999.

36. Hickford, Rev Andy, 1998, *Essential Youth,* Kingsway, Eastbourne, Page 125.
37. Article "Religion in Northern Ireland" in Brierley, Dr Peter, *Irish Christian Handbook,* 1995/96 edition, 1994, Christian Research, London, Table 4, Page 24.
38. Data supplied by the BBC Information & Analysis Department, and taken from *Religious Trends* No 2 (op cit Item 10).
39. Data from Brierley, Peter, *Prospects for the Nineties, Results of the English Church Census,* MARC Europe, London, 1991.
40. 1982 data from, Evans, Rev Byron and Brierley, Peter, *Prospects for Wales,* 1983, Bible Society and MARC Europe, London; 1995 data from Gallacher, Dr John, Challenge to Change, 1997, Bible Society, Swindon, Wiltshire.
41. 1984 and 1994 data from respectively MacDonald, Rev Fergus and Brierley, Peter, *Prospects for Scotland and Prospects for Scotland 2000,* 1985 and 1995, National Bible Society of Scotland, Edinburgh and MARC Europe (1985) or Christian Research (1995), London.
42. 1983 data from Kaldor, Dr Peter, *Who goes Where? Who doesn't care?,* 1987, Lancer, New South Wales, Australia; 1996 data from Kaldor, Dr Peter et al, Build My Church, 1999, Open Book Publishers, Adelaide, South Australia.
43. Keith Danby, Chief Executive of STL at a Christian Research Briefing held at St Luke's Church, Bolton, Lancashire, 23rd September 1998.

5: Minority Boosting

Now for some good news! In at least two denominations, the Church of England and the Methodists, ethnic minorities have specific recognition. The Committee on Black Anglican Concerns in the Church of England published a survey on black Anglican participation in 1992[1]. In 1995 its name was changed to the Committee for Minority Ethnic Anglican Concerns so as to represent those other than black[2]; a separate Association of Black Clergy has representatives on this Committee. A report published by the Methodists in 1985 specifically looked at Black Methodists[3].

There may well be other like studies or committees in other denominations. The interdenominational Centre for Black and White Christian Partnership was one sponsor of the ECAS survey, in which the opportunity was taken to ask for the ethnic composition of individual congregations so that a national picture might be obtained, and to do this not just for the large black Christian community but all ethnic groups. The same division of ethnic groups was used as in the 1991 Population Census which first asked a question on ethnic status, although some of the individual groupings were merged since their representation in the Christian community is relatively small. This meant that white people were also asked for ethnic status, but the various white nationalities were not differentiated; we did not find, for example, how many Irish there are amongst Catholic attenders.

Similar information was not collected in previous studies so overall trend information is not available.

Ethnic minorities

The overall results were encouraging. 88% of English churchgoers in 1998 were white, which means that 12% came from other ethnic backgrounds. As the population of England is 94% white and 6% from elsewhere, this means that in our church congregations there is double the proportion of other ethnic groups as exist generally in the country. Given the disastrous start to the welcome English churches gave to Caribbean and West African immigrants in the 1950s, this is encouraging news. Of course many of these groups worship in their own ethnic churches, but there is now a very considerable mixture in many congregations, with black people in white congregations for example and white people in black congregations.

In detail, the overall results were:

Table 36: Ethnic breakdown of church attendance, 1998

Group	Number	Percentage	National percentage
White	3,274,600	88.1	93.8
Black	268,600	7.2	1.9
Indian	54,700	1.5	3.0
Chinese	54,300	1.5	0.3
Other Asian	36,300	1.0	0.4
Other non-White	26,200	0.7	0.6
TOTAL	**3,714,700**	**100.0**	**47mn (=100%)**

The "Black" group includes the black Caribbeans, Africans and others. The "Indian" group includes Pakistanis and Bangladeshis as well as Indians. The "Chinese" group also includes Koreans and Japanese. It may be seen that of the total of 440,100 non-white church attenders on an average Sunday, three-fifths, 61%, are black, and the other two-fifths, 39%, are spread across the other ethnic categories. A quarter, 25%, are either Indian or Chinese.

The final column in Table 36 gives the national proportions of the various ethnic groups. It is obvious that the blacks, coming in the main from Christian countries in the West Indies and West Africa, are much more likely to be Christian. The other groups tend to come from non-Christian countries. There are fewer Christian Indians (and Pakistanis and Bangladeshis) who are Christian from their proportion in the population, but there are many more Asians who are Christian. This is almost certainly due in great part to the work of the Chinese Overseas Christian Mission and the many Korean churches in this country who especially focus on those coming from their own culture. Perhaps an Overseas Indian Christian Mission needs to be formed!

Ethnic variations by denomination

How do these different ethnic groupings vary by denomination? Table 37 gives the detail:

Table 37: Percentage of ethnic church attendance by denomination, 1998

Denomination	White	Black	Indian	Chinese	Asian	Other	Total (=100%)
Anglican	90.4	5.9	1.3	1.3	0.7	0.4	980,600
Baptist	87.7	7.8	0.9	1.6	1.2	0.8	277,600
Catholic	88.4	4.9	2.3	1.5	1.7	1.2	1,230,100
Independent	88.3	6.1	1.7	1.8	1.2	0.9	161,600
Methodist	94.3	3.9	0.5	0.9	0.2	0.2	379,700
New Churches	92.3	4.9	1.0	1.2	0.3	0.3	230,500
Orthodox	96.4	0.4	–	–	2.8	0.4	25,200
Pentecostal	64.8	32.4	1.0	0.7	0.4	0.7	214,600
United Reformed	93.7	4.3	0.7	0.9	0.2	0.2	121,700
Other denoms.	71.3	18.5	1.7	6.7	0.7	1.1	93,100
OVERALL	**88.1**	**7.2**	**1.5**	**1.5**	**1.0**	**0.7**	**3,714,700**

The denominations with fewest from other ethnic backgrounds than white are the Orthodox (because while many of them are not English at least originally, they are nearly all white), Methodist, United Reformed and New Churches. Those with most are the Pentecostals, a third of whom are black, and "other denominations", the category where all the various churches for overseas nationals are located. This latter has a high black percentage because of the many independent black churches and is also high amongst the Chinese because it is in this group that the Chinese and Korean churches will be found.

Half of all the Indian Christians in England are Catholic, reflecting the many Catholics in India. Likewise a third of all the Chinese and Korean and Japanese are Catholic, three-fifths of all the other Asians, and half of all other non-whites.

The actual number of black Anglicans reflected in the above Table is 58,200, a number about double the 27,200 counted in the 1992 report[4], and this despite an overall decrease of 16% in Anglican churchgoing in these 6 years. This considerable increase in black attendance probably comes from their switching from their own black denominations rather than a large number of black conversions through white congregations. The percentage of black Christians in Anglican churches was five times greater than the proportion in the 1990-1995 General Synod![5]

While the change in ethnic minority numbers overall are not known this experience of growth may suggest that ethnic minority church attendance is growing in England, as it has been for example in the United States[6] and Canada.

The number of black people in English Methodist churches, 14,600, is lower than the 16,000 counted in 1985. However Methodist attendance has dropped 32% from 559,000 people in 1985 to 380,000 in 1998, so that the black proportion has increased from 3% to 4%.

The total of 269,000 Black Christians is made up as follows:
- 70,000 Pentecostals
- 61,000 Catholics
- 58,000 Anglicans
- 22,000 Baptists
- 17,000 Other denominations
- 15,000 Methodists
- 11,000 New Churches
- 10,000 Independent churches, and
- 5,000 United Reformed.

Figure 28 shows the total proportions of non-whites in Table 37 by denomination:

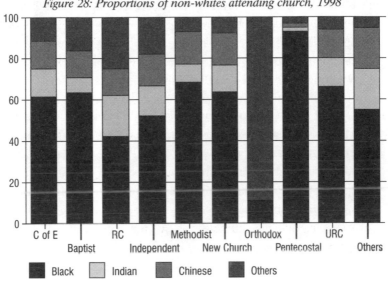

Figure 28: Proportions of non-whites attending church, 1998

Ethnic variations by churchmanship

How do the ethnic groupings vary by churchmanship? Table 38 gives details:

Table 38: Percentage of ethnic church attendance by churchmanship, 1998

Churchmanship	White	Black	Indian	Chinese	Asian	Other	Total (=100%)
Anglo-Catholic	91.1	7.4	0.5	0.5	0.3	0.2	177,600
Broad	95.3	2.3	0.7	1.3	0.3	0.1	352,400
Catholic	85.5	6.2	2.9	2.0	2.0	1.4	980,000
Evangelical	85.0	10.6	1.1	1.9	0.8	0.6	1,391,300
Liberal	93.6	4.3	0.9	0.5	0.4	0.3	425,500
Low Church	93.5	4.0	0.8	0.8	0.4	0.5	275,400
Others	89.2	8.3	1.5	0.3	0.8	0.3	112,500
Evangelical: Broad	93.7	4.4	0.7	0.8	0.1	0.3	217,900
Evangelical: Mainstream	86.0	10.1	1.0	1.8	0.6	0.5	645,500
Evangelical: Charismatic	80.2	13.8	1.5	2.3	1.3	0.9	527,900
OVERALL	**88.1**	**7.2**	**1.5**	**1.5**	**1.0**	**0.7**	**3,714,700**

This Table has a much more even spread of figures than Table 37 suggesting that churchmanship is less important than denomination in ethnic attendance. Nevertheless Table 38 shows that it is the Evangelicals, especially the Charismatics, and the smaller denominations and Anglo-Catholics who have an above average proportion of black people attending their churches. The Catholics are particularly strong with Indians and Chinese and other Asian and non-white people. Charismatic Evangelicals are strong with the Chinese and other Asian and non-white people also.

Those from Broad, including Broad Evangelical, churches, Liberals and Low Churches have the least involvement with ethnic minorities.

Ethnic variations by region

Ethnic variations by region are shown in Table 39. Note that in this Table, Greater London is split between Inner and Outer London. The first column of figures gives the total percentage of non-white people in the population of that region; churchgoers exceed the percentage every time.

Table 39: Ethnic church attendance by region, 1998

Region	N-W % pop.*	White	Black	Indian	Chinese	Asian	Other	Total (=100%)
North	1.3	95.6	1.4	0.9	1.1	0.9	0.1	225,100
Yorks/Humb.	4.4	93.0	4.2	1.2	0.7	0.7	0.2	286,400
North West	4.0	93.8	3.0	1.6	0.8	0.4	0.4	556,800
East Midlands	4.7	90.5	6.3	1.1	1.1	0.3	0.7	260,800
West Midlands	7.2	88.6	8.8	0.6	0.9	0.4	0.7	363,000
East Anglia	2.1	94.8	2.8	0.8	0.8	0.5	0.3	162,400
SE (North)	4.6	91.3	4.4	1.6	1.4	0.8	0.5	386,900
Inner London	25.6	48.8	37.4	2.8	3.6	4.1	3.3	239,700
Outer London	16.9	73.2	15.2	3.3	5.0	2.2	1.1	378,200
SE (South)	2.1	94.1	2.7	1.0	0.7	0.9	0.6	479,000
South West	1.4	96.0	1.8	0.9	0.5	0.4	0.4	376,400
OVERALL	**5.5**	**88.1**	**7.2**	**1.5**	**1.5**	**1.0**	**0.7**	**3,714,700**

*Non-whites as percentage of the regional population

Table 39 shows the importance of London for the ethnic minorities! Apart from the East and West Midlands which have about the average overall proportion, the rest of the country has only about half the ethnic percentages that attend church overall. The difference is made up by the dominance in Greater London.

Over half those attending church in Inner London are from ethnic minorities! Whilst the huge proportion of these are black, all the other groups are strongly represented, especially the other Asian and non-white. In Outer London again the percentage from all ethnic minorities is about double the average, though the Chinese are well represented – there are quite a few Korean churches in London also.

The black dominance in Inner London is large. They are three times the size of all the other groups put together. A third of all black attendance in England is in Inner London. Three out of every 8 going to church in inner London are black. Inner London is the black "mecca" of church attendance (as it is of black people in the population). The 6,000 strong Kingsway International Christian Church is but 7% of the total!

Those from black African, Caribbean and other areas are important in Outer London also, though not to the same extent. Here they are a third more again than all the others put together. A fifth of all black church attendance is in Outer London. One in every 7 going to church in Outer London is black.

While the black dominance is important, it should also be noted that half the Indians attending church do so in Greater London, twice as many more in Outer than Inner. The Chinese are however more widely dispersed throughout the country, although a third of all Chinese church attendance is still in Greater London, again twice as many in Outer as in Inner London. Half of all other Asian (equally split between Inner and Outer) and non-white (twice as many more in Inner than Outer) church attendance is also in Greater London.

These variations follow the ethnic patterns of living across England[7]. Many of the ethnic minorities live in the East and West Midlands, but most of course in London. However the proportion of black people attending church in inner London, 37%, exceeds their proportion in the general inner London population fivefold.

SUMMARY

1 1 person in 8 attending church in England is from an ethnic minority.
2 This proportion is double that in the population generally.
3 Black people account for three-fifths of all the ethnic minorities.
4 A third of all Pentecostals are black, and a sixth of the smaller denominations.
5 Black Anglicans have doubled in numbers between 1992 and 1998.
6 Two-thirds of all black churchgoers are Pentecostal, Catholic or Anglican.
7 Just over half of all church attendance in Inner London is ethnic minority.
8 3 in 8 attending church in Inner London are black, 1 in 7 in Outer London.
9 A half of all Indian church attendance is in Greater London, and a third of all Chinese.
10 The geographical variation of churchgoing ethnic minorities follows general national variations.

NOTES

1. Special Report *"Black Anglicans in England"* in the Church of England Yearbook, 1995, London, Page 178. Other relevant reports are Wilkinson, Renate, *A Chance to Change, Black Anglicans and the Church of England in the Diocese of Birmingham in 1983,* July 1984; Stone, Dr Maureen, *Black Churches in Britain, A Sociological Study,* University of Surrey, 1985; Hume, Cardinal Basil, *With you in Spirit?,* Advisory Group on commitment to the Black community, May 1986; Kerridge, Roy, *The Storm is Passing Over, a look at Black Church in Britain,* 1995, Thames and Hudson, London.
2. See for example the Annual Reports of the Committee published as General Synod Papers.
3. Walton, Heater, *A Tree God Planted,* June 1985, Black People in British Methodism, Ethnic Minorities in Methodism Working Group, Division of Social Responsibility, Methodist Church, London.
4. Op cit (Item 1), Page 178.
5. Davie, Dr Grace, and Short, Christopher, Church of England General Synod 1990-1995, 1995, *Analysis of membership,* GS Misc 464, Central Board of Finance of the Church of England, London.
6. Article by Oscar Romo, "Ethnic Church Growth and the Southern Baptist Convention" in *Urban Mission*, Philadelphia, United States, Volume 16, Number 3, March 1999, Page 27.
7. For maps illustrating this dispersion, see Brierley, Dr Peter, *Religious Trends* No 1, 1998/1999, 1997, Paternoster Publishing, Carlisle, and Christian Research, London, Figures 4.5.1-4.

6: Changing our Beliefs

Beliefs are crucial for motivation, for learning, for action and for vision. The rather odd word "churchmanship" is used as a collective noun to describe the various words by which church people describe their beliefs, much as political parties are described as "left" or "right". The making of new descriptions knows no end, but in the 1998 English Church Attendance Survey the decision was taken to maintain the same groups as used in the 1989 English Church Census. How these were initially chosen, and the ways in which the boxes ticked on the form are totalled to give the requisite categories are described elsewhere.[1]

The answers to the various questions in the ECAS study broken down by churchmanship are given in the other chapters, and are not repeated here. But as the question was asked in 1989 as well as in 1998 the opportunity can be taken to see how churchmanship has changed in these nine years. The interaction of denomination and churchmanship is also considered here.

One key assumption behind the figures is worth repeating however. The forms, both in 1989 and 1998, were sent to the minister responsible for each church with the request that they answered them on behalf of their congregation. The results are applied to each church, thus "this is a liberal church", and all in their congregation are assumed to be the same. This is a patently false assumption, but one has to assume in the absence of more detailed information that the pluses and minuses cancel each other out over the entirety of a whole denomination, churchmanship or region.

Changing church proportions

Table 40 repeats the proportions of the designations given in 1989 and adds those for 1998, the three evangelical groups at the end being a breakdown of the total evangelical component.

Table 40: Churchmanship of churches, 1989 and 1998

	Anglo-Catholic	Broad	Catholic	Evangelical	Liberal	Low Church	Others	Evangelical: Broad	Evangelical: Mainstream	Evangelical: Charismatic	Total (=100%)
1989 %	5	16	16	35	14	12	2	11	11	13	38,607
1998 %	5	13	16	38	12	12	4	9	16	13	37,717

The proportion of Broad and Liberal churches has decreased and the proportion of Evangelical and Others has increased. The Broad Evangelical churches have likewise decreased; the growth amongst the Evangelical churches is in the Mainstream churches not Charismatic. The Others are those ticking the "Other" box on the form and either leaving it blank or entering a description which is not translated into something else.

The fact that the proportion of Others has doubled is interesting. The large majority, 74%, left the "please specify" line blank or simply repeated their denomination. This perhaps suggests either they did not know which description to tick or, much more likely, they felt all of the designations to be improper labels for their position, but they could or would not give any alternative. Does this imply that these kinds of churchmanship labels are becoming increasingly anachronistic as some feel denominational labels already are? If so, the number is growing, though the proportion is still small.

76 different descriptions were offered by the remaining 26% who

did give an alternative. The most frequent were Reformed (17%), Non-Conformist (9%), Central (7%), Middle of the Road (7%), Ecumenical (5%), Fundamental (4%) and Eclectic (3%). Some which occurred just once or twice were: All Ages, Civic, Dead (!), Fellow Pilgrims, Holiness, Inornate, Liturgical, Loving Fellowship, Modern, Multi-cultural, Non-creedal, Nondescript, Prayer Book, Revival (only one in the whole of England!), Sabbatarian, Urban Youth and Word of Faith. Two key words used by up to half a dozen churches were Post-evangelical and Seeker friendly.[2]

The major items from Table 40 however are the decline in two linked important categories – the Broad and Liberal churches – and the growth in mainstream evangelicalism.

Churchmanship by denomination

Table 41 shows the estimated numbers of churches in 1989 and 1998 broken down by churchmanship and denomination.

There is a large amount of information in Table 41, but it is relatively easy to read the key movements in churchmanship over the last 9 years from it. These are as follows:

- There has been a large increase in the number of Mainstream Evangelical Anglican churches largely at the expense of Liberal ones. It is not that one has moved into the other, but rather that many Liberal churches have become, say, Broad, and many Broad churches have become Mainstream Evangelical.

- There has likewise been an increase in Baptist Mainstream Evangelical churches, with Broad and Charismatic Evangelicals decreasing (against an increasing number of Baptist Evangelicals).

Table 41: Churchmanship by denomination in churches, 1998

		Anglo-Catholic	Broad	Catholic	Evangelical	Liberal	Low church	Others	Evangelical: Broad	Evangelical: Main	Evangelical: Charismatic	Total
Angli-can	89	1,965	3,776	2,292	2,929	2,934	2,149	328	1,474	328	1,127	16,373
		−3%	−5%	+15%	+23%	−26%	0%	−16%	+5%	+219%	−11%	−1%
	98	1,902	3,570	2,631	3,589	2,163	2,149	277	1,542	1,045	1,002	16,281
Baptist	89	–	107	–	1,965	127	117	23	444	983	538	2,339
			−37%		+5%	−5%	+13%	+65%	−24%	+31%	−20%	+3%
	98	–	67	–	2,055	121	132	38	337	1,289	429	2,413
RC	89	–	–	3,709	38	39	–	38	–	–	38	3,824
		n/a	n/a	−16%	+184%	+105%	n/a	+642%	–	n/a	−26%	−1%
	98	40	150	3,101	108	80	10	282	–	80	28	3,771
Inde-pendent	89	82	165	124	2,250	248	165	63	160	1,540	550	3,097
		−31%	−92%	−98%	−18%	−57%	−21%	+33%	−12%	−3%	−60%	−28%
	98	50	14	3	1,855	106	131	84	140	1,494	221	2,243
Meth-odist	89	0	1,550	67	2,225	1,078	1,618	202	1,483	472	270	6,740
		n/a	−40%	+13%	−1%	+17%	+4%	−59%	−23%	+76%	−18%	−7%
	98	19	925	76	2,196	1,266	1,676	82	1,142	833	221	6,240
New	89	–	–	–	1,006	–	–	20	5	26	975	1,026
			n/a		+40%	n/a	n/a+1180%		+60%	+192%	+36%	+63%
	98	–	1	–	1,413	2	1	256	8	76	1,329	1,673
Orth-odox	89	3	3	4	–	–	1	103	–	–	–	114
		−67%	−67%	+50%			n/a	+143%				+126%
	98	1	1	6	–	–	0	250	–	–	–	258
Pente-costal	89	–	19	9	1,817	19	19	68	48	300	1,469	1,951
			−89%	−22%	+8%	+163%	+37%	−6%	n/a	+78%	−3%	+8%
	98	–	2	7	1,956	50	26	64	0	535	1,421	2,105
URC	89	–	319	–	403	623	284	52	269	66	68	1,681
			−31%		0%	+2%	+4%	−69%	−14%	+58%	−1%	−7%
	98	–	219	–	401	634	294	16	230	104	67	1,564
All others	89	–	117	–	1,008	190	88	59	307	629	72	1,462
			−60%		−18%	+5%	−7%	−78%	−65%	+3%	0%	−20%
	98	–	47	–	827	200	82	13	106	649	72	1,169
Total	89	2,050	6,056	6,205	13,641	5,258	4,441	956	4,190	4,344	5,107	38,607
		−2%	−18%	−6%	+6%	−12%	+1%	+42%	−16%	+41%	−6%	−2%
	98	2,012	4,996	5,824	14,400	4,622	4,501	1,362	3,505	6,105	4,790	37,717

- Independent churches have seen a considerable drop in Charismatic Evangelical, Broad and Liberal churches, and lost nearly all of their Catholics.

- There has been a significant decrease in Broad and Broad Evangelical Methodist churches, but an increase in Mainstream Evangelicals and Liberal churches (the only denomination to have a major increase in the latter).

- There has been a major increase in Mainstream Evangelical Pentecostal churches. The figures hide what has happened – a switch in about a quarter of white Pentecostal churches from being Charismatic to Mainstream, and a compensating increase almost equal to it of new black Charismatic Pentecostal churches. This switch may be because a number of Pentecostal churches wish to disassociate themselves from the churches who have experienced the Toronto Blessing, probably all of whom would call themselves Charismatic.

- The URC has lost some Broad, Broad Evangelical and Liberal churches but gained some Mainstream Evangelical ones.

- Other churches have seen a drop in the number of Broad Evangelicals.

- The main decline in Broad churches is amongst the Methodists.

- Both Broad and Charismatic Evangelicals have declined and Mainstream gained. The Broad decline is especially seen amongst the Methodists, the Charismatics amongst the Anglicans, Baptists and Independents, offset by New Church gains.

- There are fewer Liberal churches amongst the Anglicans, and Independents, but more among the Methodists.

- The Low Churches have kept remarkably the same, and "Others" also, which include the Orthodox and now many New Churches.

Individual churchmanship changes

Mention has already been made of the changing churchmanship of Pentecostal churches. A few other changes are also worth mentioning.

While the number of Evangelical churches has grown by 759 churches, 726 of these are from new Baptist, New Church or Pentecostal churches. The balance of 33 extra Evangelical churches are from 2,355 churches not previously calling themselves Evangelical who now do, and 2,322 churches who used to call themselves Evangelical but now don't. In other words, while many new church plants may be evangelical, there is in addition a massive movement amongst Evangelical churches as to what their theological position is. One church in 6 which was Evangelical in 1989 was not Evangelical 9 years later. In some churches this will be because the minister has moved and one of a different persuasion has come, and they (incorrectly) completed the form from their own position rather than that of the congregation. For how many this may be so is not known, but suppose half. That still leaves one Evangelical church in 12 leaving their evangelicalism in 9 years, 130 every year, or just over 2 a week.

To what do they move? Half, 53%, have registered in 1998 as Low Church; 20% as Liberal, 18% as Broad, and 9% Catholic or Anglo-Catholic.

From where do newly registering Evangelical churches come? Five in every 8, 62%, come from the "all other" designation category, in other words, those whose position was perhaps more fluid or who were in the position of thinking through specifically what they should be.

Of the remainder, a fifth, 20%, were formerly Broad or Liberal, some of whom presumably have moved because their minister has changed. One in seven, 15%, were previously Low Church.

Evangelicals aren't the only ones to change! Relatively few Anglo-Catholics or Catholics have changed. A third, 32%, of those who were Broad are now Liberal, and 25% Low Church. A third, 30%, of those who were Liberal are now Broad, suggesting that these two terms are becoming interchangeable. A fifth, 20%, of those who were Liberal are now Low Church. Two-fifths, 40%, of those who were Low Church are now Broad or Liberal.

Why these changes took place is not specifically known. It may be that a new minister gives a different connotation from the previous minister to the meaning of a particular churchmanship classification. Another reason, as one evangelical leader suggested, is that they are too word-based, and cited the example of a Greek Orthodox girl who had been to the Easter Saturday night service where she said she had stood for 3 hours with her hands in the air while the priest shouted, "He is Risen!" and found it "an unforgettable experience".

People not churches

As churches are of different sizes, what are the numbers of church people by churchmanship and denomination, and how have these changed over the last 9 years? Tables 42 and 43 give similar detail to Table 41 but for Sunday church attendance, Table 43 giving the detail for Evangelicals in their constituent parts.

Naturally some of the features of Table 42 will be similar to those emerging from Table 41. Note however in addition:

- The huge confusion in categorisation, seen by the large increase in "Others" and the fact that every denomination has seen high turbulence in this category. It suggests that new categories are needed.

Table 42: Sunday church attendance by churchmanship and denomination, 1998

		Anglo-Catholic	Broad	Catholic	Evangelical	Liberal	Low church	Others	Total
Angli-	89	151,300	230,000	158,700	331,300	246,900	129,800	18,300	**1,266,300**
can		*-7%*	*-51%*	*-66%*	*+2%*	*-20%*	*+1%*	*-70%*	*-23%*
	98	140,300	113,300	54,300	338,600	198,000	130,700	5,400	**980,600**
Baptist	89	100	14,600	600	225,300	19,700	9,300	1,300	**270,900**
		n/a	*-42%*	*n/a*	*+7%*	*-9%*	*-6%*	*-23%*	*+2%*
	98	–	8,500	–	241,400	18,000	8,700	1,000	**277,900**
RC	89	5,200	30,000	1,677,900	6,700	10,000	400	12,700	**1,715,900**
		+296%	*+341%*	*-45%*	*+691%*	*+325%*	*+1100%*	*+353%*	*-22%*
	98	20,600	132,200	919,400	53,000	42,500	4,800	57,600	**1,230,100**
Inde-	89	20,700	25,700	16,100	192,700	24,400	13,400	5,500	**298,500**
pend-		*-26%*	*-77%*	*-91%*	*-34%*	*-83%*	*-51%*	*-73%*	*-46%*
ent	98	15,400	5,800	1,400	126,700	4,200	6,600	1,500	**161,600**
Meth-	89	600	123,300	5,900	171,500	102,400	97,400	11,200	**512,300**
odist		*+100%*	*-46%*	*-31%*	*-22%*	*-24%*	*-3%*	*-82%*	*-26%*
	98	1,200	66,400	4,100	133,400	78,300	94,300	2,000	**379,700**
New	89	–	–	–	165,300	–	–	1,700	**167,000**
			n/a		*+30%*	*n/a*	*n/a*	*+700%*	*+38%*
	98	–	200	–	215,300	1,100	300	13,600	**230,500**
Ortho-	89	200	400	200	–	–	–	11,500	**12,300**
dox		*-50%*	*0%*	*+250%*				*+109%*	*+105%*
	98	100	400	700	–	–	–	24,000	**25,200**
Pente-	89	200	1,000	6,300	220,900	1,800	1,400	5,100	**236,700**
costal		*n/a*	*-70%*	*n/a*	*-10%*	*+161%*	*+214%*	*+27%*	*-9%*
	98	–	300	–	198,700	4,700	4,400	6,500	**214,600**
URC	89	–	31,600	1,400	22,000	68,600	22,700	3,000	**149,300**
			-39%	*-93%*	*+15%*	*-13%*	*-25%*	*-83%*	*-18%*
	98	–	19,400	100	25,200	59,500	17,000	500	**121,700**
All	89	–	4,400	400	94,700	6,100	6,100	1,900	**113,600**
Others			*+34%*	*n/a*	*-38%*	*+215%*	*+41%*	*-79%*	*-18%*
	98	–	5,900	–	59,000	19,200	8,600	400	**93,100**
Total	89	**178,300**	**434,000**	**1,867,500**	**1,430,400**	**479,900**	**280,500**	**72,200**	**4,742,800**
		0%	*-19%*	*-48%*	*-3%*	*-11%*	*-2%*	*+56%*	*-22%*
	98	**177,600**	**352,400**	**980,000**	**1,391,300**	**425,500**	**275,400**	**112,500**	**3,714,700**

*Table 43: Sunday church attendance
by evangelical churchmanship and denomination, 1998*

| Denomination | Year | Evangelical | | | TOTAL |
		Broad	Mainstream	Charismatic	Evangelical
Anglican	1989	163,800	23,200	144,300	**331,300**
		-23%	+320%	-21%	**+2%**
	1998	126,400	97,500	114,700	**338,600**
Baptist	1989	49,200	109,000	67,100	**225,300**
		-66%	+42%	+4%	**+7%**
	1998	16,900	154,400	70,100	**241,400**
Roman Catholic	1989	-	2,900	3,800	**6,700**
			+1179%	+318%	**+691%**
	1998	-	37,100	15,900	**53,000**
Independent	1989	34,300	97,300	61,100	**192,700**
		-73%	-3%	-62%	**-34%**
	1998	9,200	94,500	23,000	**126,700**
Methodist	1989	122,400	25,600	23,500	**171,500**
		-54%	+125%	-14%	**-22%**
	1998	55,800	57,500	20,100	**133,400**
New Churches	1989	1,100	35,900	128,300	**165,300**
		-64%	+108%	+9%	**+30%**
	1998	400	74,700	140,200	**215,300**
Orthodox	1989	-	-	-	**-**
	1998	-	-	-	**-**
Pentecostal	1989	4,700	30,500	185,700	**220,900**
		n/a	+109%	-27%	**-10%**
	1998	-	63,700	135,000	**198,700**
United Reformed	1989	5,500	4,000	12,500	**22,000**
		+2%	+235%	-50%	**+15%**
	1998	5,600	13,400	6,200	**25,200**
All others	1989	33,600	56,200	4,900	**94,700**
		-89%	-6%	-45%	**-38%**
	1998	3,600	52,700	2,700	**59,000**
TOTAL	**1989**	**414,600**	**384,600**	**631,200**	**1,430,400**
		-47%	*+68%*	*-16%*	*-3%*
	1998	**217,900**	**645,500**	**527,900**	**1,391,300**

- The change in the Roman Catholic classification. Whereas Mass attendance decreased 22% 1989-1998, the decrease in the "Catholic" classification has been twice that, much of it by Roman Catholics. Instead they have seen large increases in all other classifications. Perhaps the awareness of these other groups has grown in the 1990s as a consequence of the reforming of the old Council of Churches into Churches Together which included the Roman Catholics for the first time.

- The Anglican Anglo-Catholic drop is less than might be expected after the decrease in the number of Anglo-Catholic priests due to their disagreement with the ordination of women. What seems to have happened is the members who left in support of the priests have rejoined their original church. Some of the priests have joined smaller splinter Continuing Anglican churches, but these in the main have very small congregations. Writing in 1996, Kenneth Leech wrote, "Today Anglican Catholics are more divided, fragmented and confused than they have been for a long time"[3], and gave four reasons to support his statement. Even if true of leadership, the above numbers suggest that it is less true of lay people in 1998.

- Evangelical growth, while small, has occurred amongst the Anglicans, Baptists, Roman Catholics, New Churches and United Reformed, and is therefore fairly widespread. Independent evangelicalism would have declined even if switching from Independents to New Churches had not occurred. It is the basic drop in the Methodists, Pentecostals and the other smaller denominations (including the Salvation Army which is entirely evangelical) which account for the overall decline. The increase in evangelicalism amongst Roman Catholics is not unique for England; it is also happening in North America, where in one study[4] a fifth attending Mass weekly described themselves as evangelical.

• The strengths of the three main groups in each denomination are shown in Figure 29. The Orthodox are not shown as they are almost entirely "Other". It should be noticed that the proportions by people are different from proportions by churches since different types of churches are different sizes.

Figure 29: Churchmanship by denomination, 1998

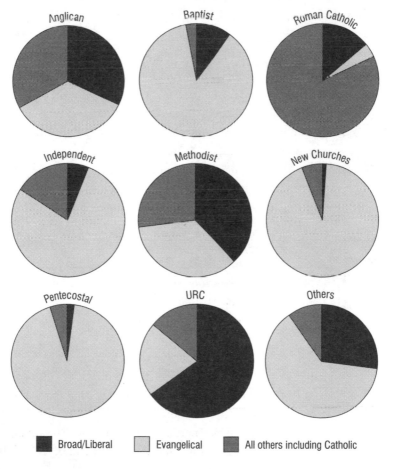

- The growth in Mainstream Evangelicalism is across all denominations except the Independent and other smaller denominations, in which it declined only marginally. The same is true for the decline in Broad Evangelicalism, except for a small increase in the United Reformed Church. The Charismatics have grown amongst the Baptists, Roman Catholics and New Churches only, but declined elsewhere.

The sheer weight of so many numbers makes Tables 42 and 43 confusing. Table 44 gives both sets of information, but this time as percentages of the denominational total, and the dominance of each churchmanship in each denomination can thus be more readily seen.

Table 44: Percentage of denominational attendance by churchmanship, 1998

		Anglo-Catholic %	Broad %	Catholic %	Evangelical %	Liberal %	Low church %	Others %	Evangelical: Broad %	Evangelical: Main %	Evangelical: Charis. %	Total (=100%)
Anglican	89	12	18	13	26	20	10	1	13	2	11	1,266,300
	98	14	11	6	35	20	13	1	13	10	12	980,600
Baptist	89	–	5	–	83	7	4	1	18	40	25	270,900
	98	–	3	–	87	7	3	0	6	56	25	277,900
RC	89	–	–	98	–	1	–	1	–	–	–	1,715,900
	98	2	11	75	4	3	0	5	–	3	1	1,230,100
Inde-pendent	89	7	9	5	65	8	4	2	12	33	20	298,500
	98	9	4	1	78	3	4	1	6	58	14	161,600
Meth-odist	89	0	24	1	34	20	19	2	24	5	5	512,300
	98	0	17	1	35	21	25	1	15	15	5	379,700
New	89	–	–	–	99	–	–	1	1	21	77	167,000
	98	–	0	–	93	1	0	6	0	32	61	230,500
Ortho-dox	89	2	3	2	–	–	–	93	–	–	–	12,300
	98	0	2	3	–	–	–	95	–	–	–	25,200
Pente-costal	89	0	0	3	93	1	1	2	2	13	78	236,700
	98	–	0	–	93	2	2	3	–	30	63	214,600
URC	89	–	21	1	15	46	15	2	4	3	8	149,300
	98	–	16	0	21	49	14	0	5	11	5	121,700
Others	89	–	4	0	84	5	5	2	30	50	4	113,600
	98	–	6	–	63	21	9	1	4	56	3	93,100
Total	89	4	9	39	30	10	6	2	9	8	13	4,742,800
	98	5	9	27	37	12	7	3	6	17	14	3,714,700

The shaded boxes in Table 44 indicate where the number of people in that category has changed by at least 50,000 over the nine years to 1998. They highlight the main movements that have occurred.

Figure 30 shows the proportions for Evangelicals in Table 44, treating each group as totalling 100%, to illustrate which denominations have larger percentages of Broad, mainstream and Charismatic.

Figure 30: Composition of the Evangelical groups by denomination, 1998

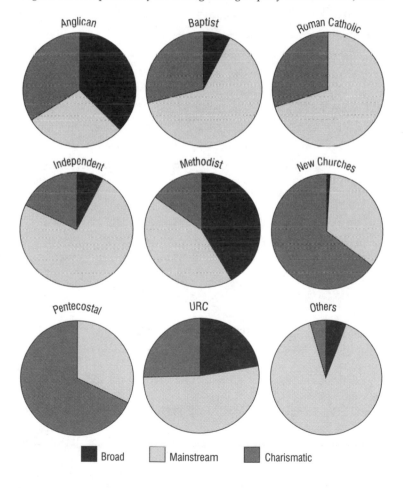

SUMMARY

1 The number of Broad and Liberal churches has especially declined over the years 1989 to 1998.

2 The number of Evangelical churches have grown because of the growing number of Evangelical Mainstream churches.

3 Both the numbers of Broad and Charismatic Evangelical churches have declined.

4 Many more churches are now unwilling or unable to give a churchmanship statement.

5 About a quarter of Pentecostal churches have switched from being Charismatic to Mainstream.

6 There was a large increase in the number of Mainstream Evangelical Anglican churches.

7 Two Evangelicals churches a week turn from their evangelicalism; two non-Evangelical churches a week become evangelical.

8 Broad and Liberal are becoming more interchangeable terms.

9 The Evangelical growth is spread throughout most of the larger denominations.

10 The Anglican Anglo-Catholics have not declined as much as might have been expected given their turbulence during the 1990s.

Notes

1. See Brierley, Peter, *'Christian' England*, Page 155f., Prospects for the Nineties, Pages 15,16, 1991, MARC Europe, London, and *Religious Trends* No 2 2000/2001, 1999, HarperCollins and Christian Research, London, Page 12.2.

2. A full list is available from Christian Research at the address at the front of this book.

3. Leech, Rev Kenneth, *The Sky is Red*, 1997, Darton, Longman and Todd, London, Page 220.

4. Article in *Religion Watch*, New York, Volume 14, Issue 10, September 1999, Page 3.

7: Movement to Midweek

Attendance at church worship services is not confined to Sundays! When the minister of a large Anglican church was asked in 1998 what would be the main difference in church life in 2003 he said, "We will be meeting for worship on Thursday evenings. Sunday morning will just be for those who like singing." When this was mentioned to a group of Methodists meeting for Easter People at Bournemouth at Easter 1999 many agreed with it, "even if the theology seems a bit wrong", as one put it.

Mid-week services

On a Council Estate in Dartford, Kent an Anglican vicar started a service on Wednesday mornings. Matins at 9.30 am. Whoever would come? About 25 mums regularly attend, the time convenient so they can arrive after they've dropped their children at school. They do not come to church on Sunday, because their husbands don't want to be tied to looking after the children in their absence.

Such stories could be multiplied many times. The English Church Attendance Survey asked respondents if they had a regular mid-week worship service. 42% replied YES. On the assumption the same applies to the churches which didn't take part, then that means that almost 16,000 churches across England are holding regular services during the week. The average attendance is 21 people.

That is a total attendance of 335,000 people, or 0.7% of the pop-

ulation. Of course some of these will also come on Sunday, and we
have no way of knowing how many who come mid-week do so. Since
12% of churchgoers attend twice on Sunday, might it be reasonable
to suggest that double that percentage, 25%, come twice during the
week, that is, to a mid-week service and on Sunday? That would
mean, if true, that 75% who come mid-week don't come on Sunday,
or 250,000 people, or 0.5% of the population.

The 42% figure varies as shown in Table 45:

Table 45: Percentage of churches holding Mid-week worship services (M)
by denomination, churchmanship and region, 1998

Denomination	M %	Churchmanship	M %	Region	M %
Anglican	51	Anglo-Catholic	78	North	42
Baptist	45	Broad	36	Yorks/Humberside	41
Catholic	31	Catholic	51	North West	39
Independent	59	Evan: Broad	36	East Midlands	37
Methodist	22	Evan: Mainstream	52	West Midlands	44
New Church	23	Evan: Charismatic	41	East Anglia	40
Orthodox	46	Evangelical:Total	44	S E (North)	37
Pentecostal	66	Liberal	42	Gr London	51
URC	19	Low Church	26	S E (South)	43
Others	34	Others	10	South West	41

Pentecostals, Independent churches and Anglicans are the three
denominations where more than half hold a mid-week service. This
is especially true for the Anglo-Catholic and Catholic churches
where it is presumably a mid-week Eucharist or Mass. More mid-
week services are held in churches in Greater London than in other
parts of the country. The first column in Table 45 is illustrated in
Figures 31 and the third in Figure 32:

Figure 31: Percentage of churches holding mid-week worship services
by denomination, 1998

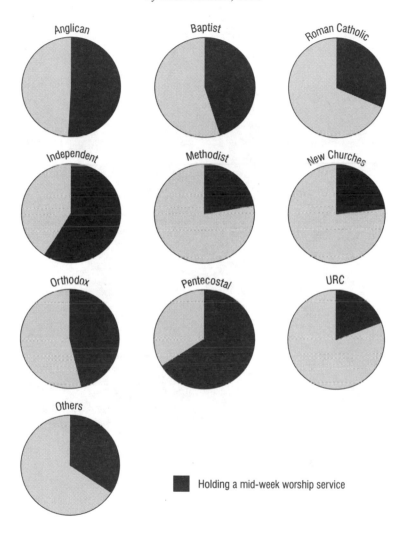

Holding a mid-week worship service

Figure 32: Percentage of churches holding mid-week worship services by region, 1998

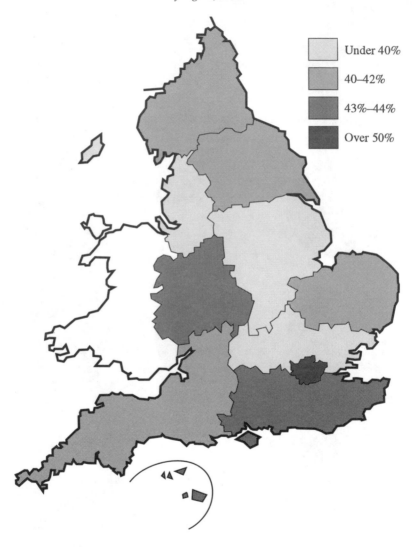

The average size of these services also varies, and these are given in Table 46:

Table 46: Number attending Mid-week worship services (NoM)
by denomination, churchmanship and region, 1998

Denomination	NoM	Churchmanship	NoM	Region	NoM
Anglican	15	Anglo-Catholic	16	North	24
Baptist	20	Broad	13	Yorks/Humberside	19
Catholic	35	Catholic	29	North West	21
Independent	21	Evan: Broad	17	East Midlands	19
Methodist	17	Evan: Mainstream	21	West Midlands	20
New Church	48	Evan: Charismatic	31	East Anglia	17
Orthodox	44	Evangelical:Total	24	S E (North)	20
Pentecostal	31	Liberal	14	Gr London	31
URC	16	Low Church	14	S E (South)	21
Others	21	Others	21	South West	17

The New Churches, Orthodox and the Catholics have the largest congregations on average, explaining why it is the Charismatic and Catholic churchmanships have most people mid-week. London has the best attended services regionally, followed by the North.

In 1979, 37% of churches held at least one mid-week meeting, and the overall attendance was 76 people[1]. However these were any kind of mid-week meetings, such as house groups, prayer meetings, etc. as well as worship services, whereas the ECAS question was specific. Nevertheless some of the 37% would have included worship services, though the percentage is unknown, and would have been lower. It means then that over the two decades in between the percentage of churches holding mid-week *worship* services has increased. Perhaps by 2003 many more churches will be having mid-week worship services!

Not all extra services are necessarily held on church premises. ASDA in Liverpool for example open half an hour later one morning a week so that their staff can attend communion first. Many homes for the elderly hold services for their residents. But as we only sent the form to churches we can only answer on behalf of services held in church. The above numbers of and attendances at worship services undertaken each week across England are therefore likely to be conservative rather than exaggerated.

Youth Services

It is likely that only a small minority of participants at mid-week services will be young people. This is partly because of opportunity (many are at work or school), partly because of the kind of service, and partly because a number of churches are now offering a special "youth service", many during the week. The ECAS form asked if churches held a regular Youth worship service. One in seven, 14%, did, with an average attendance of 43.

If these numbers are averaged out over all the churches in the country, then this would mean that there were 220,000 young people coming to such services. There will always be some of these who will also come to "normal" services on Sundays, but experience suggests the majority probably do not. Suppose only 10% also come on Sunday – a completely estimated figure. Some churches will hold such services every week, but probably the majority will be monthly; suppose the average turns out to be one every 3 weeks. Putting this together would then suggest that...

- On average an extra 67,000 young people are attending Youth services each week.
- If the majority of these are aged 15 to 19, then this would mean that the number of young people actually attending worship services is one third more than those who come on Sunday, that is, a quarter of teens connected with church are coming to their own special service.
- It is equivalent to an extra 0.4% of the population attending a "church" service once a month.

- Whilst the numbers of teenagers attending church on Sunday has still fallen overall since 1989, three-fifths of this fall is due to special services being provided for them, and their switching from normal services to these services.
- These Youth services are then very successful in retaining young people, which naturally implies that more should be encouraged.

All this suggests that the huge emphasis that many churches and parachurch organisations have put into reaching and keeping teenagers in the 1990s has been successful. Whilst earlier (Table 27) it was shown that 270 young people aged 15 to 19 leave the church each week, in reality perhaps 160 of these are instead diverting to worship or other spiritual activities specially suited to them.

These comments have assumed that all those coming to Youth worship services are aged 15 to 19. In reality some will be younger, and some will be in their 20s, but as the age of those attending was not requested, it isn't known. However the success of these services does suggest that ascertaining exactly what kind of services they are, the age and gender of those who come, the actual frequency with which they are held, their degree of independence from the main church, etc. would be worth investigating in further research.

Some of those attending these services are students at college. With Local Authority grants now withdrawn, most students search for work to support their studies. Not a few work at weekends, including Sunday. When one such student was asked why he didn't attend church on Sunday, he simply replied, "I go to the Youth Service every Thursday."

The 14% figure of churches holding these services varied as might be expected, and these are given in Table 47 across the three main parameters, though again denomination was the most heterogeneous:

Table 47: Percentage of Youth worship services (Y)
by denomination, churchmanship and region, 1998

Denomination	Y %	Churchmanship	Y %	Region	Y %
Anglican	14	Anglo-Catholic	15	North	10
Baptist	16	Broad	10	Yorks/Humberside	12
Catholic	5	Catholic	8	North West	15
Independent	19	Evan: Broad	15	East Midlands	12
Methodist	10	Evan: Mainstream	19	West Midlands	15
New Church	17	Evan: Charismatic	25	East Anglia	13
Orthodox	15	Evangelical:Total	20	S E (North)	13
Pentecostal	39	Liberal	14	Gr London	18
URC	13	Low Church	9	S E (South)	14
Others	21	Others	3	South West	14

The Pentecostal churches hold the most regular Youth worship services, almost three times as many as all the other denominations.

After that the most holding them were the Other, smaller denominations, and the Independent churches. The Roman Catholics, Methodists and United Reformed Churches had the smallest proportions but churches of all denominations hold some. More churches in Greater London held these services than in other areas, with the smallest percentage in the North.

Table 45 is illustrated in Figures 33 and 34:

Figure 33: Percentage of churches holding regular youth worship services
by denomination, 1998

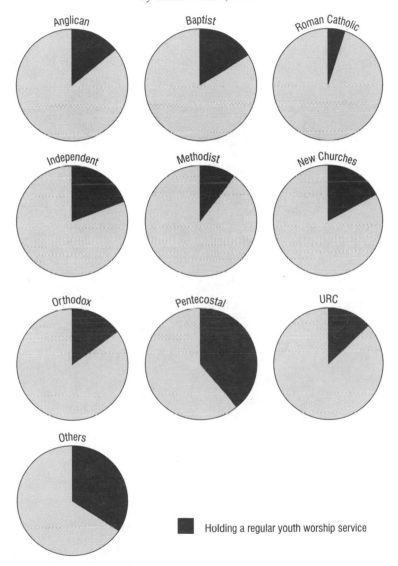

Holding a regular youth worship service

Figure 34: Percentage of churches holding regular youth worship services by region, 1998

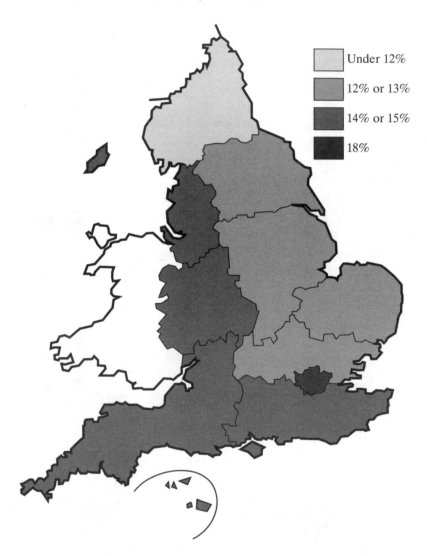

The size of these services varied as shown in the next Table:

Table 48: Number attending Mid-week services (NoY)
by denomination, churchmanship and region, 1998

Denomination	NoY	Churchmanship	NoY	Region	NoY
Anglican	53	Anglo-Catholic	50	North	33
Baptist	39	Broad	48	Yorks/Humberside	39
Catholic	83	Catholic	69	North West	49
Independent	32	Evan: Broad	44	East Midlands	40
Methodist	42	Evan: Mainstream	35	West Midlands	38
New Church	41	Evan: Charismatic	40	East Anglia	35
Orthodox	60	Evangelical:Total	38	S E (North)	45
Pentecostal	26	Liberal	45	Gr London	46
URC	41	Low Church	41	S E (South)	47
Others	15	Others	34	South West	43

The Roman Catholics may have the smallest percentage of Youth worship services, but where they do have them they are on average twice the size of everyone else's.

Youth Leaders

What is driving this move to Youth worship services? One reason is the explosion in the number of churches appointing full-time, and therefore paid, Youth Leaders, Youth Pastors, Youth Ministers, or some such title meaning someone whose prime responsibility is the young people's work in their local church. I have heard ministers say they would prefer having a Youth Minister to an Assistant Minister or Curate. The prime reason is the realisation in many churches that youth work is of crucial importance and in the 1990s requires professional leadership, whereas previously it has largely been left to enthusiastic and well-intentioned volunteers with limited time and sometimes limited experience.

The Oxford Brookes University Youth Ministry is the largest supplier of qualified church Youth Leaders in the country, each studying "youth, community and applied theology". The course began in 1998 with 30 students; it had 60 in 1999 and expected to continue to attract more[2]. Other organisations like Youth for Christ and St Johns College, Nottingham, to name but two, also started another similar course in 1998[3].

The English Church Attendance Survey asked churches if they had a "full-time salaried youth worker". 21% said they did, one in every 5. It is possible some churches misunderstood the question; some Anglican churches for instance gave the name of their curate as s/he had youth work as their prime responsibility. But taking the percentage at its face value would suggest about 7,900 full-time youth leaders in English churches in 1998.

The questionnaire also asked if the church had a person responsible for children's work with those under 12. These would not normally be full-time or salaried people, but volunteers working with children in the Sunday School or other activities. Nearly three churches in five, 59%, had such a person.

Did a church have a person responsible for young people's work, working with those aged 12 and over? Four in every 9 did, 44%. Of course churches had these people in different combinations, as follows:

- 36% only a Children's Leader
- 22% only a Young Person's Leader
- 18% only a paid Youth Leader
- 21% with both a Children's Leader and Young Person's Leader
- 2% with both a Children's Leader and paid Youth Leader
- 1% with just a Young Person's Leader and paid Youth Leader
- 0.5% with all three

This is the good news. The flip-side of the above statistics is that 41% of churches, two in every five, had no-one who was responsible for any kind of youth or children's ministry. Several wrote on their forms, "We have no Sunday School now".

One 1998 survey[4] of 900 evangelical churches showed that their average Sunday School had 30 children, though 50% had under 24, and 17% under 11. Only 10% had more than 60. In this context "Sunday School" meant all the young people of whatever age attached to the church. More worryingly, some Sunday Schools had no children in a particular age-group: two churches in five had no creche, and over half the churches in this sample had no young people aged 15 to 18. The actual percentages are illustrated in Figure 35:

Figure 35: Percentage of churches with no children in a particular age-group

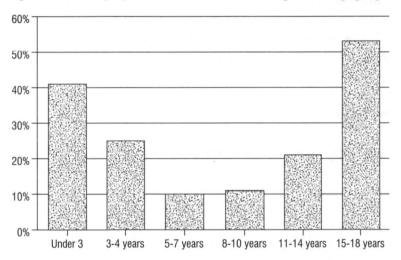

In the mid 1990s Christian Research was asked to undertake some research for a well-known Christian youth organisation. We wrote to a wide sample of churches asking if they would be willing to distribute a questionnaire to 10 of their young people aged 12 to 18. We had hundreds of churches writing back saying they did not have 10 young people of these ages to give them to.

It is of course essential that churches preach the good news to everyone. But today there is an added urgency to taking the gospel to young people – not just attracting them to the Kingdom, but also seeking to keep them once there. "Reaching and Keeping Teenagers" was the subject of a 1993 survey[5].

One of the problems with Youth Services is the integration of those who attend into "normal" church life subsequently. Many have enjoyed attending Youth Services but are not now attending church; "I tried it once," they said. Hence the importance of encouraging rigorous personal spirituality.

Often appointing a Youth Leader will mean fundamental change to a church life. A Youth worship service may be part of this. Such services usually mean fewer Family Services in a church. Not all churches are willing for such change. One Cambridge minister said, "We don't want change, just more families please." But as we enter the 21st century, we have to change if we are to keep in business, as it were. Having a Youth Leader is one way which many churches are following.

Youth Work

Why should churches put such emphasis on youth work? Few churches have the resources to take advantage of all the opportunities open to them, so they have to prioritise. Work amongst children and young people is important because:

- It is still true that 70% of those who come to faith do so before the age of 20[6], a percentage which has changed very little since 1968 (76%)[7]. However it is older teenagers being converted in the 1990s whereas it was younger teenagers in the 1960s[8].
- The absence of Christian exposure and the consciousness of the emptiness of materialism makes younger people more open to the genuine story of Christianity. It is the story which attracts them, as the Bible Society's Open Book project emphasises[9].
- A quarter of young people today experience their parents

divorce, or grow up in a single parent family; some of these are Christian. This often makes young people realistic enough to see the need for help from something beyond themselves.

If young people are the most receptive group in Britain today, what of students, at an age when if they were going to leave the church they are most likely to do so[10]? Christian work amongst students has a long history in the UK, both by evangelicals and non-evangelicals. A number of new organisations to help students have started in the 1980s or 1990s.

Christian Union numbers can vary quite dramatically – for instance there were 15,000 students at Reading University in 1999 and a Christian Union of 230. In Luton University with 10,000 students, there was a Christian Union of 40[11]. The type of University, the style of leadership, the degree of external support are all important factors. Do older established Universities tend to have large Christian Unions (because of longer tradition) than the newer Universities? Does the influence of large local evangelical churches tend to have any influence on the size of Christian Unions?

Fringe attenders

Many churches have halls or other buildings which are available for community use. Many Play Groups, Drop in Centres, Mothers & Toddlers Groups, Senior Citizens, Luncheon Clubs etc. use such for their mid week activities. Many sports are played in such facilities. Many meetings are held in such premises. Some of these are specifically church connected but others are not so, and the church premises are simply being hired out.

The English Church Attendance Survey asked churches whether their premises were used for such church run activities, and if so, roughly how many children and adults were involved in them each week, asking specifically for "fringe" people who attended these events but did not regularly attend worship services. The question specifically asked that outside organisations who hired or used church premises should be excluded.

Four churches in every 9, 45%, have premises from which mid-week church run activities are undertaken. On average such activities reached 37 adults (over 15 years of age) and 33 children per week. That works out at 2.4% of the entire population who are "involved" with the church at least to the extent of attending some mid-week activity – 1.2 million people. That is a large number, with a huge potential for evangelism. How may the opportunity it provides best be taken?

Table 49: Percentage of Fringe mid-week activities (F)
by denomination, churchmanship and region, 1998

Denomination	F %	Churchmanship	F %	Region	F %
Anglican	44	Anglo-Catholic	43	North	43
Baptist	65	Broad	36	Yorks/Humberside	46
Catholic	12	Catholic	24	North West	51
Independent	58	Evan: Broad	62	East Midlands	39
Methodist	51	Evan: Mainstream	60	West Midlands	43
New Church	33	Evan: Charismatic	59	East Anglia	38
Orthodox	23	Evangelical:Total	60	S E (North)	48
Pentecostal	50	Liberal	47	Gr London	50
URC	59	Low Church	45	S E (South)	50
Others	46	Others	7	South West	38

As with previous questions, the percentage and numbers attending vary. The Baptists, United Reformed Church, and Independents were the three denominations most likely to be using their premises for mid-week activities. Evangelicals were much more likely than non-Evangelicals to be using their premises in this way (60% to 36%). More churches in the North West, Greater London and South East (South) used their premises in this way than in other regions.

The numbers attending these activities are shown in the next

Table, where the first figure is the average number of adults, and the
second children.

Table 50: Number attending Fringe mid-week activities (NoF)
by denomination, churchmanship and region, 1998

Denomination	NoF	Churchmanship	NoF	Region	NoF
Anglican	66:36+30	Anglo-Catholic	61:33+28	North	76:42+34
Baptist	83:40+43	Broad	63:34+29	Yorks/Humberside	66:35+31
Catholic	67:40+27	Catholic	65:38+27	North West	92:57+35
Independent	57:27+30	Evan: Broad	79:41+38	East Midlands	60:32+28
Methodist	77:41+36	Evan: Mainstream	68:34+34	West Midlands	67:35+32
New Church	61:30+31	Evan: Charismatic	80:41+39	East Anglia	59:32+27
Orthodox	94:54+40	Evangelical: Total	75:38+37	S E (North)	67:35+32
Pentecostal	57:26+31	Liberal	71:39+32	Gr London	91:49+42
URC	65:31+34	Low Church	60:34+26	S E (South)	71:35+36
Others	80:54+26	Others	59:35+24	South West	60:32+28

The Orthodox, Baptist and other smaller denominations have the
largest numbers of fringe people, as do the Evangelicals and those in
the North West and Greater London.

It must not be thought that these are the only fringe people to contact church people. Not so! There is much other activity, seen, as
just one example, in the numbers of people who go to Christian
Retreat Houses for refreshment. "Many who come here have no
allegiance to any Church," wrote one Warden. "Some come on business conferences and experience a different atmosphere and a different way of looking at life. Some come looking for peace and relief
from stress. They do not fit into a parish system and are put off by
much of what they see of church life."[12]

Alpha Courses

One of the more successful ventures launched in the 1990s has been
the Alpha courses, through the ministry of Rev Nicky Gumbel based
in an evangelical Anglican church, Holy Trinity, Brompton, in Central

London. These take people through the major articles of Christian belief in the context of a friendly meal and relaxed atmosphere where anyone can ask any question. Other like courses, such as Emmaus, are also available. Alpha courses began in 1992 and have since grown worldwide, with attendance numbers as shown in Table 51[13]:

Table 51: Alpha courses worldwide

Year	Number of registered courses	Number attending	Average number per course	Cumulative total of attenders
1992	5	100[1]	20[1]	100
1993	200	4,600	23	4,700
1994	750	22,100	29	26,800
1995	2,500	76,400	31	103,200
1996	5,000	156,750	31	259,950
1997	6,500	283,440	44	543,390
1998	10,500	435,980	42	979,370
1999	20,860[2]	834,420[1]	40[1]	1,813,790

[1]Estimate   [2]Taking HTB's own estimate for the first six months, and increasing it by 50% for the full year

In 1999 just under half of Alpha courses, 47%, were held in the UK, and almost a quarter, 24%, in Canada and the United States. In the early 1990s, many of those going to a course would have already been attending church, as church people wanted "to see what it was like" before inviting their friends. That will be less true in the later 1990s. Suppose half of Alpha attendance in 1999 was non-church people; then that amounts to just under 200,000 people, or 0.4% of the population.

So where does all this take us?

If we summarise the figures given thus far in this book we get a picture something like the following:

- 7.5% of the population attend church every Sunday
- 2.7% more attend on a Sunday once a month
- 0.5% of the population attend a mid-week service at church
- 0.4% attend a Youth worship service once a month
- 0.4% of the population attended an Alpha course in 1999
- 1.9% of the population watch *Songs of Praise* but do not attend church on Sunday
- 2.4% of the population attend mid-week church activities but do not attend church on Sunday

There is unlikely to be much overlap between these figures, which total 15.8% of the population, but suppose there is some, say 0.8%, leaving 15% – twice the percentage who actually attend church every Sunday. It is also certain that much church activity is omitted since it is unmeasurable.

These 7 figures say two things: Firstly, Sunday church attendance is only half (literally half!) the story about church in England. Secondly, a fair slice of church life is outside the regular church altogether, and therefore not controllable by church hierarchies; perhaps that's as it should be.

How are these figures changing? The first is decreasing, but the next four are increasing. *Songs of Praise* is static at present, and the last is unknown. It has not been measured before. Since the first is the largest, probably therefore overall we are seeing a decrease, but at nothing like the rate suggested in the second chapter.

What do these figures say about measuring church people?

- They seem to support the suggestion already made that monthly rather than weekly would be an appropriate period of time to measure things.
- They also indicate the importance of including non-Sunday activity, and since this could be open to wide mis-use, it may be best if it was confined to attendance at mid-week worship services, whether for adults or as special youth events.

- Thirdly, we must look at Christian activities which are not directly church services, and recognise their importance. Only two are mentioned above – Alpha courses and *Songs of Praise*. The estimated 150,000 Christian people who attended Easter People, Spring Harvest or Stoneleigh Bible Weeks in 1999, for example, another 0.3% of the population, are not included above. Nor the thousands who marched in *March for Jesus* in 1999 or watched it on TV[14]. Nor is the impact of the *Jesus* video, of which 138,000 were distributed in the UK in the period January 1995 to September 1999. 60,000 of these were just in the months June to September 1999.[15] At this level of interest it is estimated the total number distributed could reach 220,000 by the end of 1999. If all these were only seen by one non-church person, that's another 0.4% of the population.

However let us not be complacent. The main measurement of "church" is bound to be Sunday church attendance, since Christians acknowledge the first day of the week, and one of the Ten Commandments is quite explicit about the seventh day, though keeping it holy does not necessarily equate to attending a church service! Sunday attendance figures are therefore bound to be carefully scrutinised by the media, and churches should not avoid giving these figures as well as others. This would also then give continuity with past information.

Healing Services

The ECAS study also asked churches if they held one of four types of healing services. This question was kindly sponsored by the Christian Healing Mission. Two-thirds, 67%, did not. The other third did, as follows:

- 36% Laying on of hands, etc. at times other than regular healing services
- 23% Regular Healing services
- 23% Counselling style healing ministry by minister/leader
- 19% Counselling style healing ministry by lay people

These overlapped, with each church who had at least one of these having on average three of these four forms of ministry. They also varied by denomination, churchmanship and region as shown in the following Tables:

Table 52: Healing services in English churches by denomination, 1998

Denomination	Laying on of hands %	Healing services %	Minister counselling %	Lay people counselling %	NO healing services %
Anglican	36	29	19	16	56
Baptist	41	12	23	23	61
Catholic	26	31	30	13	89
Independent	44	13	24	20	76
Methodist	26	33	27	15	80
New Church	37	11	24	28	50
Orthodox	26	19	48	6	56
Pentecostal	38	17	24	21	19
URC	29	33	19	18	74
Others	31	18	33	18	77
OVERALL	**36**	**23**	**23**	**19**	**67**

Roman Catholics and Methodists were least likely to have healing services, or perhaps more didn't answer the question than others! Pentecostals had by far the most, four churches in every five, showing their traditional emphasis on healing. New Churches, Anglicans and Orthodox followed next.

The Independents and Baptists have most laying on of hands, and the United Reformed and the Methodists regular healing services. Counselling by minister was most seen in the Orthodox churches, and by lay people in New Churches.

Table 53: Healing services in English churches by churchmanship, 1998

Churchmanship	Laying on of hands %	Healing services %	Minister counselling %	Lay people counselling %	NO healing services %
Anglo-Catholic	39	34	19	8	56
Broad	33	35	21	11	73
Catholic	32	31	26	11	77
Evan: Broad	34	30	21	16	62
Evan: Mainstream	41	18	24	17	68
Evan: Charismatic	37	14	23	26	28
Evangelical:Total	38	20	23	20	53
Liberal	30	41	19	10	70
Low Church	29	32	23	16	76
Others	27	31	26	16	94
OVERALL	**36**	**23**	**23**	**19**	**67**

The large majority, three-quarters, 72%, of the charismatic churches have healing services. Mainstream Evangelicals prefer the laying on of hands, Liberals healing services, Catholics-counselling by ministers, Charismatics-counselling by lay people.

Table 54: Healing services in English churches by region, 1998

Region	Laying on of hands %	Healing services %	Minister counselling %	Lay people counselling %	NO healing services %
North	35	27	22	16	77
Yorks/Humberside	37	24	22	18	68
North West	32	26	23	19	68
East Midlands	38	19	24	19	71
West Midlands	34	25	23	18	63
East Anglia	39	22	21	18	68
S E (North)	36	23	22	20	65
Gr London	36	22	23	19	59
S E (South)	36	23	22	19	61
South West	35	25	23	18	67
OVERALL	**36**	**23**	**23**	**19**	**67**

The variations between the regions are small and insignificant.

Technical helps

The ECAS study asked if churches had a fax number. Only 1.7%, or 1 in every 60, did. However I suspect this is deliberately greatly under reported to save being targetted by unwanted "junk" faxes. Orthodox churches had the most (5.1%), followed by New Churches (3.2%) and Pentecostal churches (2.5%). Because of their dominance in the last two groups, Charismatics had the most fax machines (3.1%), followed by the Catholics (2.5%). Churches in East Anglia had the fewest (0.5%), and those in Inner London the most (3.3%).

*"I know I never come to church,
but I often visit your website!"*

The survey also asked if churches had an email number. These were again almost certainly under reported (or the form was completed by someone other than the minister who did not know it). Overall 1.2% did, with the New Churches (3.0%) and the Orthodox (2.6%) having the most, and the United Reformed (0.3%) the least. Again the Charismatics had the most (2.7%). Churches in the North had the fewest (0.3%) and those in South East (South) the most (1.7%).

Did ministers have email, irrespective of whether their churches had? Only 1.3% of ministers gave an email number at the time of the survey, autumn 1998. Again New Church leaders had the highest percentage (5.9%), followed again by the Orthodox (2.6%), with the Anglicans (0.9%), smaller denominations (0.4%), and Roman Catholics (0.3%) the lowest. Again the Charismatics had the most (2.6%). Ministers in the North had fewest (0.5%), those in Inner London the most (2.3%).

More than one church

Five ministers in 6, 82%, look after just one church. One sixth of ministers, 18%, looked after more than one church. Of these 18%,

- 62% were responsible for 2 churches,
- 21% were responsible for 3 churches,
- 9% were responsible for 4 churches,
- 4% were responsible for 5 churches,
- 2% were responsible for 6 churches,
- 1% were responsible for 7 churches, and
- 1.5% were responsible for 8 or more churches.

A 1989 survey[16] of Methodist and Anglican churches in East Anglia showed that most ministers who looked after more than one church could cope with up to four, but after that church life (and the minister!) deteriorated.

This ECAS survey shows that 8.5% of ministers looking after 2 or more churches are in this danger zone, equivalent over all ministers to 1 in 65. The above percentages varied most by denomination and region; details are given in Table 55, where the percentages for 2 or more churches are expressed as a percentage of all those with 2 or more, in an analogous way to the above figures. The average is only the average of those looking after at least 2 churches. Thus, for example, 73% of Anglican ministers are responsible for just one church; 27% therefore look after 2 or more. Of this 27%, 62% look after 2 churches, which is 17% (27% x 0.62) of all Anglican ministers. 20% of the 27% look after 3 churches (5% of the total), and so on.

Table 55: Number of churches looked after by one minister, 1998

	Anglican	Baptist	Roman Catholic	Independent	Methodist	New Church	Orthodox	Pentecostal	URC	Others	Overall
	%	%	%	%	%	%	%	%	%	%	%
ONE only	73	92	95	96	69	95	80	95	63	89	82
2	62	85	85	85	45	79	51	77	70	77	62
3	20	10	9	13	27	13	25	11	23	15	21
4	10	2	5	2	11	4	21	6	4	5	9
5	4	2	1	–	6	2	3	3	1	1	4
6	2	1	–	–	5	–	–	1	1/2	0	2
7	1	–	–	–	2	–	–	1	1	1	1
8 or more	1	–	–	–	4	2	–	1	1/2	1	11/2
Average 2+	2.7	2.2	2.2	2.2	3.2	2.4	2.8	2.5	2.4	2.4	2.7

	North	Yorks/Humberside	North West	East Midlands	West Midlands	East Anglia	SE (North)	Greater London	SE (South)	South West	Overall
	%	%	%	%	%	%	%	%	%	%	%
ONE only	84	79	83	78	79	81	81	90	82	79	82
2	64	59	68	59	58	42	60	82	70	55	62
3	25	22	24	18	23	17	23	14	19	22	21
4	5	8	5	9	10	19	11	3	7	9	9
5	2	6	2	5	3	10	2	1	3	6	4
6	2	2	1	5	4	5	3	–	1	3	2
7	1	1	–	2	1	2	1/2	–	0	3	1
8 or more	1	2	–	2	1	5	1/2	–	1/2	2	11/2
Average 2+	2.6	2.8	2.4	2.9	2.8	3.5	2.7	2.2	2.5	3.0	2.7

The Methodists, Orthodox and Anglicans have the most ministers looking after more than one church. These are also most prevalent in East Anglia and the South West of England. Table 55 is illustrated in Figures 36 and 37.

*Figure 36: Number of churches for which ministers were responsible
by denomination, 1998*

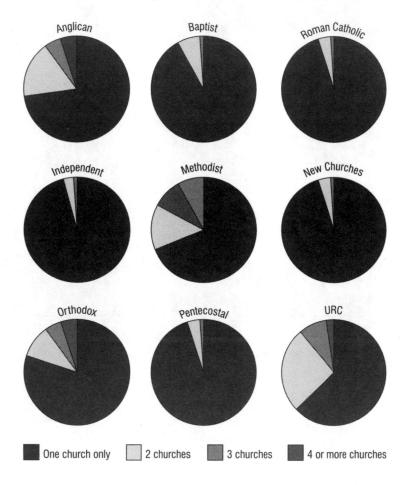

*Figure 37: Number of churches for which ministers were responsible
if responsible for at least 2, by region, 1998*

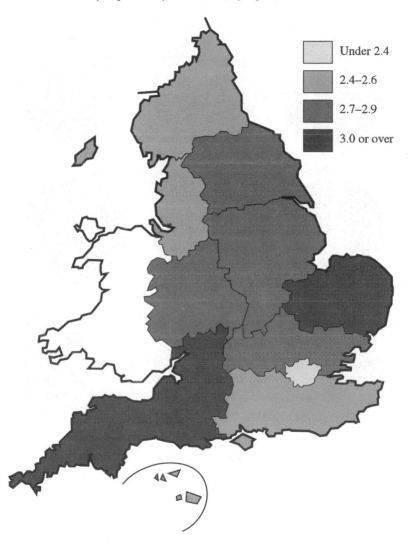

SUMMARY

1 42% of churches have a mid-week worship service with an average attendance of 21, equivalent to 0.5% of the population. Pentecostal, Independent and Anglican churches have the most.

2 This percentage has grown over the last two decades.

3 14% of churches have a youth worship service, with an average attendance of 43, equivalent to 0.4% of the population. 39% of Pentecostal churches have such services.

4 21% of churches have a full-time salaried youth worker.

5 52% of churches have no teenagers aged 15 to 18 in their congregation, and 41% no children under 3. 70% of those who come to faith do so by the age of 20; hence the urgency of children's and youth work.

6 45% of churches have fringe people coming to mid-week activities but not worship, average number 70, equivalent to 2.4% of the population. 65% of Baptist churches have such activities.

7 Sunday church attendance is only half the total activity of the church.

8 33% of churches have a healing service; 81% of Pentecostals.

9 2% of churches have a fax machine; 1% an email number. 1% of ministers are also on email.

10 One minister in six looks after at least 2 churches. The average may be 2.7 churches for these, but 8.5% of them look after 5 or more.

NOTES

1. Nason-Clark, Mrs Nancy, analyst, *Prospects for the Eighties:* Volume 2, From a Census of the Churches in 1979 undertaken by the Nationwide Initiative in Evangelism, 1983, MARC Europe, London, Page 22.
2. These were the numbers they had at their residential training week in September 1999; their leader said they had many applications.
3. Details in Wraight, Heather, editor, *UK Christian Handbook,* 2000/2001 Millennium edition, 1999, HarperCollinsReligious and Christian Research, London.
4. Unpublished survey undertaken for Scripture Union, and quoted with permission.
5. Written up in Brierley, Peter, *Reaching and Keeping Teenagers,* 1993, Monarch Publications, Crowborough, East Sussex, with Christian Research, London and CPAS, Leamington Spa.
6. *Finding Faith in 1994,* survey of 4,800 people for Churches Together in England, a summary of which was given in *Quadrant,* March 1998, Christian Research, London.
7. *Background to the Task,* 1968, Scripture Union, London, report of a survey of 4,000 people.
8. Comment by Jim Love, American Baptist evangelist in Northampton.
9. The *Open Book* project identifies five challenges to the church of which the first is to see the Bible as a story rather than a "religious book", Bible Society, Swindon, 1998 overhead transparency.
10. Op cit (Item 6).
11. Op cit (Item 8).
12. Johnson, Revd Graham, in a letter to *The Tablet,* 3rd-10th April, 1999, Page 485.
13. *Alpha News,* No 18, March-June 1999, with South Africa increased by 800 courses and United States by 1,000, per personal conversation with Rev Nicky Gumbel.
14. 50 million in 177 countries in the years 1988-1999 according to an article "Fall in for the final UK march" by Erica Youngman, *Celebrate,* March 1999, Monarch Publications, Crowborough, East Sussex.
15. Personal conversation with Agapé staff member, September 1999. See also the article by Ruth Brown "Jesus Video opens up a community", *Agapé News,* Spring 1999, Birmingham, Page 9.
16. Brierley, Peter, *More Than One Church,* 1989, report of a survey of 155 ministers responsible for 585 churches, MARC Monograph Number 27, MARC Europe, London.

8: Caring for our Heritage

The English Church Census (ECC) in 1989 was the largest survey of its kind that had then been undertaken of English church life. As well as asking about attendance, the questionnaire also asked the year in which the congregation or church had been founded. Altogether over 26,600 respondents answered this question, and most answered it in respect of the year in which the church had been built. For those congregations which did not meet in an ecclesiastical building, the year when the congregation started to meet was given.

A few in ecclesiastical buildings which had been closed and then re-opened, gave the year of re-opening, or an otherwise later date than when the building was actually built, but such numbers were small. Some churches, apart from new ones, which did not answer the ECC study gave the year they started in answer to the ECAS study, but this chapter focussing on the age of churches draws on the much large number available through the ECC for its primary analysis.

Some who did not know the actual year of construction often simply wrote "Twelfth century" or whatever; all such were treated as 1100 and likewise for other centuries. Those who gave events instead had an appropriate date substituted. As the dates analysed below are grouped into centuries or decades little is lost by a few dates not being quite accurate.

The ECC results have already been analysed and the results published[1]. That commentary is not repeated here. What is new however is an analysis of what has happened *since* 1989, and to this we give attention, together with salient comments that come from a deeper analysis of the earlier material.

The churches which responded to the ECC and to ECAS were of course churches still in existence. We simply do not know how many churches have been built, fallen into disuse and subsequently closed, apart from those started since 1985, a year the ECC also asked about. These figures of new churches cannot be assumed to give any reliable indication of church building and closure in previous decades or centuries.

Number of churches

The total number of churches in England in 1998 was 37,717. That is a large number of "outlets" – far more in fact than the total of Tesco, Sainsburys, ASDA, Woolworths, Co-op, Marks and Spencer! In commercial terms, so many churches provide a huge "presence".

This number of churches is equivalent to 1 church for every 1,320 people – about the same as for pubs. It is also twice as many as the number of Post Offices. What image do these buildings provide? How old are they?

Overview of ages of current church buildings

The Table opposite shows the huge church building programme that operated in the 11th to 13th centuries, and which still accounts for 1 in 6 (16%) of our churches in use today. The rapid expansion of the church, especially into urban areas as the Industrial Revolution got under way, in the 19th century is also seen. Three in every eight of churches today (37%) date from the 19th century.

One out of three (35%) of today's churches were built this century, which obviously means that two-thirds were built previously, rough- ly half of which were built the previous century, and the other in all the earlier times since Christianity first came to England with the Roman conquerors. That so many have survived and are still in use today is a testimony to the craftmanship that went into their building, and underlines the importance of the heritage that our churches give to the country.

Table 57: Date of foundation of current churches or congregations by century

Century	Percentage
Pre 8th	0.5
8th	0.2
9th	0.9
10th	1.1
11th	3.9
12th	6.2
13th	5.7
14th	2.4
15th	1.2
16th	0.6
17th	2.2
18th	2.8
19th	37.4
20th	34.9
Total	37,717

7,000 churches in use at the dawn of the 21st century were built before 1300! They are now all Church of England, the majority will be listed buildings, and require in some cases huge amounts of maintenance. Most are rural, many will have small congregations, with an incumbent who looks after several simultaneously. How can the church put money into people not property?

The 19th and 20th centuries

The latter half of the nineteenth century saw a huge church building programme. This was partly in response to the finding in the 1851 Population Census, the first to include a religious question, that there were not enough seats in churches should everyone in the country wish to attend. This was especially true in the urban areas to which many of the population had moved.

Figure 38: Number of churches built per century, up to 1998

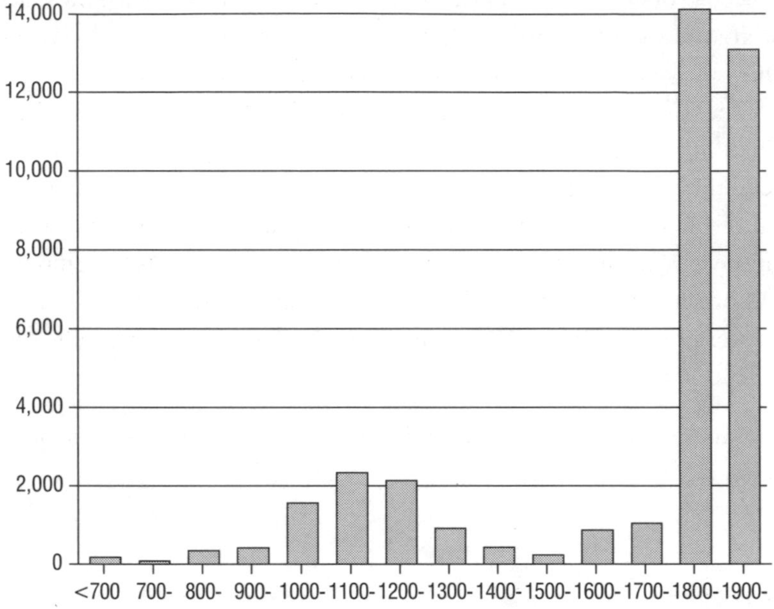

Horace Mann's Report[2] said that 1,645,000 "inhabitants of England would not be able ... to join in public worship" and suggested that some 2,000 churches be built to remedy this deficiency. His Report was published in 1854. In the next 45 years some 8,700 would be built, many times more than strictly necessary, and many therefore inevitably rarely, if ever, filled.

It was these facts that lay behind the analysis by Professor Robin Gill in his book *The Myth of the Empty Church* in which he meticulously shows that many churches in the nineteenth century were mostly empty[3]. The Victorians did not fill the churches in their church attendance.

The number of churches built in the 19th and 20th centuries was partly because of the Industrial Revolution, but also partly because of the growing population, and growing religious diversity. Roman Catholics, who had been barred from all kinds of activity since the Reformation, were allowed to build churches in 1829 and appoint

Members of Parliament in the 1840s. The Irish potato famines in the 1840s brought many refugees into the country, most of whom were Catholic and therefore needed places for worship. Figure 39 shows how the number built changed across these two centuries.

The impact of the two World Wars can be seen in the diminished building programme in the first half of the 20th century, although it could be argued that the number of new churches would diminish after the huge numbers built between 1850 and 1900. The need for more was just not there! The increase since 1975 reflects the emphasis on church planting by the Pentecostal and New Churches, but a closer examination of these years is interesting. They are graphed in Figure 40.

Figure 39: Number of churches built in England in 19th and 20th centuries

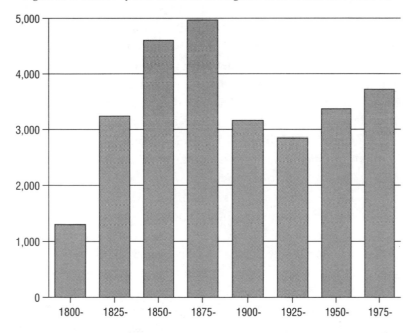

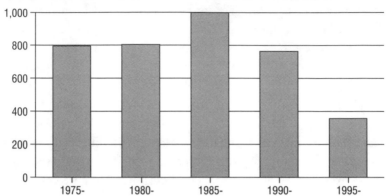

Figure 40: Number of churches built 1975 to 1998 in 5 yearly intervals

While the last bar only gives the number of churches started for 4 years rather than 5, it is obvious that the thrust of church planting has slipped quite profoundly in the 1990s from its heyday in the 1980s. The Pentecostal churches have been rethinking their strategy, and a number of New Churches have had to work through leadership issues. This internalised thinking has meant less outward emphasis on new buildings. The actual numbers are given in Table 58, and the final line makes clear the shortfall as the century closes.

The numbers built since 1985 have been carefully monitored by Rev George Lings, now based in Sheffield. Those in Table 58 agree with his figures[4]. In one article he wrote, "About 25,000 people attend Anglican church plants begun since 1977", more than the total attending in two-thirds of the Dioceses![5]

At the Challenge 2000 Conference in 1992 there was a call to start 20,000 new churches by the turn of the century. This has not come about, but nevertheless some 3,000 churches have been started since 1975 by the Free Churches.

The figures in Table 58 are net figures. More churches will have started in the period shown, some of which will have closed again. These are simply the starting dates of current surviving churches.

Table 58: Number of churches built and congregations started in 19th and 20th centuries, and every five years since 1975, by broad denominational group

Date	Anglican	Catholic	Free	Orthodox	Total	% of all
1800-1824	195	46	1,064	0	**1,305**	3
1825-1849	1,411	213	1,615	0	**3,239**	9
1850-1874	1,801	508	2,295	0	**4,604**	12
1875-1899	1,215	625	3,129	0	**4,969**	13
1900-1924	848	553	1,760	0	**3,161**	8
1925-1949	634	577	1,604	25	**2,840**	8
1950-1974	793	750	1,721	105	**3,369**	9
1975-1998	442	401	2,848	128	**3,819**	10
Total 19th & 20th	**7,339**	**3,673**	**16,036**	**258**	**27,306**	**72**
Total all centuries	**16,281**	**3,771**	**17,407**	**258**	**37,717**	**100**
Percentage 19th & 20th of total	*45%*	*97%*	*92%*	*100%*	*72%*	–
1975-1979	92	178	495	30	**795**	2
1980-1984	80	113	586	25	**804**	2
1985-1989	79	78	845	18	**1,020**	3
1990-1994	110	12	654	40	**816**	2
1995-1998	81	20	268	15	**384**	1

Churches by churchmanship

The present churchmanship of a church is not necessarily that under which the church was originally built or started, but as there is no information on the initial churchmanship, all we can do is look at the current churchmanship.

Figure 41 reflects the evangelical church plants in the 1990s, and the large number of Broad and Anglo-Catholic churches which date before the 16th century (mostly rural churches). It shows the impact of the Anglo-Catholic Oxford Movement in the second half of the 19th century (especially 1850-1874) with the number of Anglo-Catholic churches then built, and the impact of the Roman Catholic building programme in the first three quarters of the 20th century.

Figure 41: Churchmanship by age of church

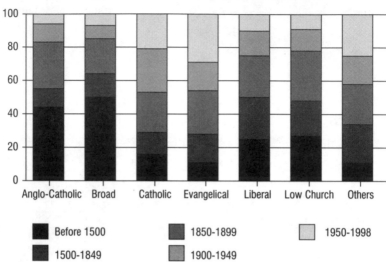

Each of the top three parts in each column in Figure 41 relate to 50 years worth of church building. They clearly indicate church-manship differences. A breakdown of the evangelical figures is given in Table 59:

Table 59: Evangelical churches by type and age of church

Period	Broad %	Mainstream %	Charismatic %	Total %
Before 1500	27	10	6	11
1500-1799	7	3	6	5
1800-1824	4	2	6	4
1825-1849	12	5	10	8
1850-1874	16	8	13	12
1875-1899	15	8	19	14
1900-1924	7	7	10	8
1925-1949	3	10	9	9
1950-1974	5	12	10	10
1975-1998	4	35	11	19
Total (=100%)	3,505	6,105	4,790	14,400
% of total	9	16	13	38

The Table shows a decline in the number of new Broad evangelical churches in the 20th century. The huge number of Mainstream churches, over 2,100, started in the last quarter of this century is a major feature of the Table.

Church openings and closures

The number of churches which have closed in the past 9 years exceeds the number which have opened. Between 1989 and 1998 1,867 churches opened but 2,757 closed, a difference of 890 churches, the difference between the 38,607 churches counted in 1989 and 37,717 churches in 1998. Details are given in Table 60. The 1,867 figure in the penultimate line is the number of churches built after 1989, and the 90 is the estimated number of these which closed.

Table 60: Church closures 1989-1998

When built	Number in 1989	Closed 1989-1998	Left in 1998
Before 1975	36,289	2,529	33,760
1975 to 1989	2,318	138	2,180
Total 1989	38,607	2,667	35,940
1989 to 1998	1,867	90	1,777
Total 1998	**40,474**	**2,757**	**37,717**

The church closures 1989 to 1998 average a rate of 6 a week, and the openings 4 per week. In the 1980s the rate of church closures was also at the average of 6 per week, and in the first half of the 1990s they continued at the same rate[6]. In other words, the rate of closure of existing churches in the final 20 years of the 20th century has remained the same – on average 6 per week.

The number of churches opening however has changed. Between 1980 and 1994 the average number opening each week was 6, thus keeping the total number of churches in the land constant. Since 1994 fewer churches have been started – an average of only 4 per week, which means that the church "stock" has declined since then.

The net effect at the close of the second millennium is that 100 churches in England are closing every year. In gross or overall numbers this means that every year 200 churches are opening but 300 are closing. Where has the energy and vision gone that went into starting 300 new churches every year, which was the rate between 1980 and 1994? What has changed in the last 5 years? Are churches starting new services in an existing facility rather than a congregation in a new facility?[7]

Opening and closing churches affects churches of all denominations. Whilst some denominations have seen many more new churches started than other denominations, like the New Churches, even here they have seen some closures. In the 1980s in England, 83% of the closures were by the Church of England and the Methodist Church. However, they jointly opened on average 27 churches per year as well.

The overall proportions by denominations based on the detailed figures for 1989 to 1998 are shown in Figure 42:

Figure 42: Percentage of churches opened and closed by denomination, 1989-1998

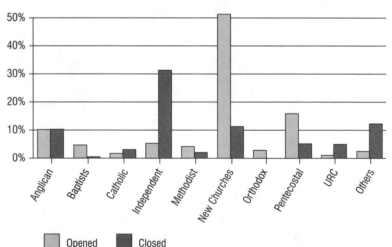

This bar chart shows where the main emphasis has been in church planting initiatives – the work of the New Churches in its various streams, the Pentecostals who have started nearly 300 churches in these 9 years, and the Anglicans who while closing more than they have opened have nevertheless still opened 239 new churches[8].

It also indicates the major denominations which are closing churches: the Independents, Methodists and the Other smaller denominations. The Methodists are essentially engaged in a rationalising policy of closing small, uneconomic and less used churches; the others tend to close because those attending, often elderly, die and the remaining congregations are unable to sustain them. The Methodists are concerned about the impact of their policy and have produced a video *Stopping the Rot!* which suggests four characteristics of newly formed churches worth emulating in others: atmosphere, language, lack of pressure and interest.

Churches by region

When were the churches built in the different parts of the country? The next Table indicates:

Table 61: Age of churches by Region of England

Date	North	Yorks/Humber	North West	East Midlands	West Midlands	East Anglia	SE (North)	Greater London	SE (South)	South West	Total Number	Total as %
	%	%	%	%	%	%	%	%	%	%		
Before 1500	14	17	7	30	22	43	28	6	26	29	8,293	22
1500-1799	7	7	6	6	4	5	7	4	4	7	2,118	6
1800-1824	2	3	4	5	3	2	4	2	4	4	1,305	3
1825-1849	9	12	13	8	10	4	6	6	5	10	3,239	9
1850-1874	16	15	16	10	11	8	10	16	12	11	4,604	12
1875-1899	17	14	18	12	11	10	9	18	12	12	4,969	13
1900-1924	10	9	11	6	7	4	8	15	9	5	3,161	8
1925-1949	8	8	8	4	7	4	8	15	8	5	2,840	8
1950-1974	9	8	11	7	10	5	10	13	10	5	3,369	9
1975-1998	8	7	6	12	15	15	10	5	10	12	3,819	10
Total (100%)	2,443	3,606	4,044	3,856	3,790	2,662	3,800	3,743	4,212	5,561	37,717	100

History can be traced in Table 61:

- The first line (before 1500) reflects the Roman occupation, and later settlement of the Norman conquerors which had less impact on the northern parts of England.

- The larger percentages for Yorkshire and the North West in 1825-1899, show where the Industrial Revolution impacted most, and the church's response to it.

- The increase in the proportion of churches being built in London from 1850 in the following 125 years reflects the population movement and denominational response to that, both as people move into Greater London and as, in the 20th century, they move into the counties around Greater London.

- The higher than average percentages in the 1900-1924 line are where the Roman Catholics concentrated their building programme at the turn of the century.

- The larger numbers in the 1950-1974 line are where churches were rebuilt after the bombings of the Second World War, especially in London.

- The final line shows the expansion of the church in the latter part of this century, especially with population movement into East Anglia and the South West, and the spread of churches for ethnic minorities, especially in the Midlands.

These figures do not necessarily reflect attendance patterns since congregation size varies in different parts of England, the rural and urban areas having fewer people per church than suburban areas.

Table 62 takes the total figures given in Table 60 and breaks them down by region. The line labelled "Closure of these" is estimated.

Table 62: Churches opening and closing by region, 1989-1998

	North	Yorks/Humber.	North West	East Midlands	West Midlands	East Anglia	SE (North)	Greater London	SE (South)	South West	Total
Total churches 1989	2,550	3,827	4,039	3,911	3,868	2,769	3,943	3,549	4,297	5,854	**38,607**
Started 1989-1998	+70	+107	+164	+124	+158	+107	+182	+565	+291	+99	**+1,867**
Closures of these	−3	−5	−8	−6	−8	−6	−9	−27	−14	−4	**−90**
Closures of pre-1989's	−174	−323	−151	−173	−228	−208	−316	−344	−362	−388	**−2,667**
Net change 1989-1998	−107	−221	+5	−55	−78	−107	−143	+194	−85	−293	**−890**
Total churches 1998	2,443	3,606	4,044	3,856	3,790	2,662	3,800	3,743	4,212	5,561	**37,717**

There are two regions where there is a positive net change over these 9 years: Greater London and the North West. Elim held a strong campaign in the North West in the early 1990s to plant more churches, and many of those started in this Region are Pentecostal. Kensington Temple in central London has also had a strong church planting programme in the 1990s and of the 454 new churches started 129 are through their work. Many of the rest are the burgeoning numbers of African and Caribbean churches and those of other ethnic minority groups in the capital to which reference was made earlier. In the London Borough of Newham for example 64 Pentecostal fellowships in 1994 had mushroomed to over 100 by 1998.[9]

The high closure programme in the South West shows the continuing policy of the Methodist Church in that region. The closing of some rural churches, often through combining with other parishes, by the Church of England partly accounts for the decline in the North, and East Anglia. Some of the Anglican closures are also in the inner city areas, as evidenced by the high numbers in the East and West Midlands, a closure policy shared with the United Reformed Church and the Methodists. Often Local Ecumenical Projects (LEPs) are created when two or three churches in an area are closed and a new one built, or three are merged into one, newly furnished, building. The main decline, however, is in the number of small independent churches, which frequently have no, or a more restricted, wider group to help them.

Figure 43a: Number of churches opening 1989-1998

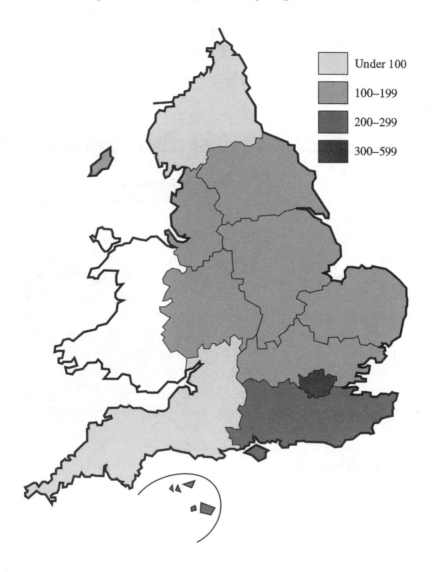

Figure 43b: Number of churches closing 1989-1998

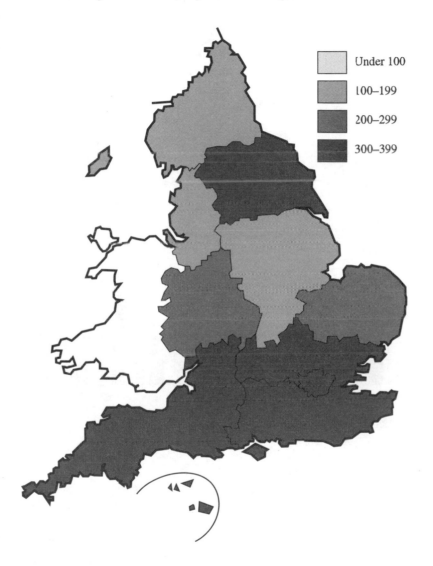

Where there was such a positive net change the number of church closures was also smaller. Could this suggest that in areas where vigorous church planting was taking place such activity acts as an inhibitor to some extent in the closure of other churches? If so, this is an interesting corollary to a church planting programme.

Figure 44 graphs the percentages of churches opening and closing in the 9 years covered by Table 62[10], and Figure 43 puts the data in map form:

Figure 44: Percentage of churches opened and closed by region, 1989-1998

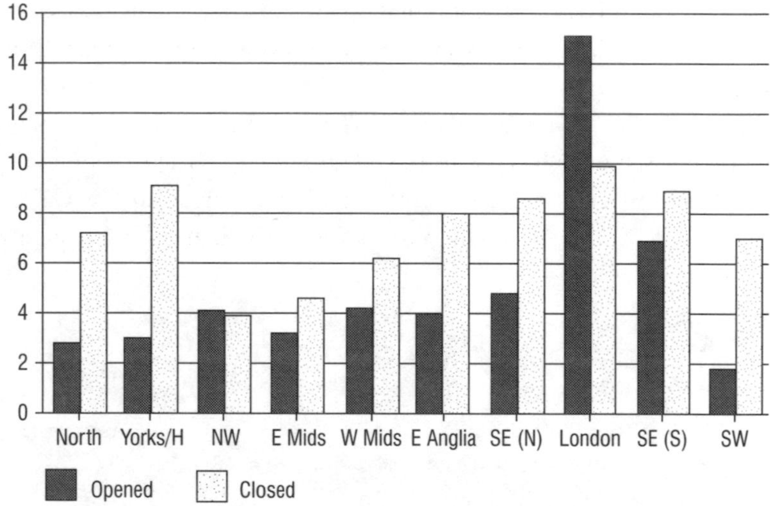

Church growth

It may be seen from Figure 43b that the many church closures take place in rural areas. This is because of "small, ageing membership. ... Pastoral ministry is lacking in many country districts with leadership being the responsibility of faithful deacons or church secretaries" as one report[11] stated. A detailed survey by the Rural Development Commission[12] found that only 39% of rural churches or chapels had a resident minister. 53% had no Sunday School[13].

It must not be thought that church closures means a complete lack of church growth. Sometimes this is happening very imaginatively, such as in the "Kairos Church from Scratch" launched by Rev Rob Warner in Wimbledon, south London, in June 1999.[14]

In the 1990s "all major denominations have come to put church planting on their agendas and most have some level of formal recognition of its significance"[15]. But many now recognise "the need to tackle the fundamental malaise of British churches – their essentially maintenance orientation"[16]. It is also important to recognise that church planting takes energy and vision, and leadership can grow weary! There is a recognition that a new initiative seems necessary, but as yet this does not appear to be generally happening, apart from individual efforts.

In 1995 a world-wide survey of growing churches by a German, Christian Schwarz, has led to the "Natural Church Development"[17] emphasis, which is being supported and encouraged in the UK by the British Church Growth Association[18]. It focuses on 8 quality characteristics:

- Empowering leadership
- Gift-orientated lay ministry
- Passionate spirituality
- Functional structures
- Inspiring worship service
- Holistic small groups
- Need-orientated evangelism
- Loving relationships.

The different types of church plant have been helpfully specified[19] by Rev Stuart Murray who teaches church planting at Spurgeon's College:

- Pioneer Planting (mission orientated in a new area),
- Replacement Planting (or replication),
- Sectarian Planting (on the basis of denomination), and
- Saturation Planting (on the basis of numbers of churches per population).

It is the Pioneer Planting types which need to be the focus of fresh dreams and ideas.

Local Ecumenical Projects (LEPs)

As noted above, some church closures come about through the rationalisation of several churches of different denominations in one area. These may be 2 or more denominations using the same buildings at different times, but usually it means a merger of services and activities. The resulting church is often called a Local Ecumenical Project or LEP. Many LEPs were set up in the 1970s and 1980s, and in 1989 an analysis of the various types was made based on 1,138 LEPs[20]. They continue to increase in number, but much more slowly than hitherto – about 20 new LEPs a year were made in the 1990s.

While they can be between up to 7 denominations, the majority are between two. In 1989 69% were between 2, in 1998 76%. The largest combinations are:

- Methodist and URC,   26% in 1989, 36% in 1998
- Methodist and Anglican,   25% in 1989, 22% in 1998
- Other two-way combinations   17% in 1989, 19% in 1998
- Three-way combinations,   17% in 1989, 11% in 1998
- Four-way combinations,   12% in 1989, 7% in 1998
- Five or more combinations,   3% in 1989, 5% in 1998

Listed Buildings

English Heritage kindly sponsored four questions in the ECAS study. Their answers may be of interest to others. One of them related to whether church buildings were officially listed. Exactly one-third, 33%, were. About a quarter, 23%, of those replying did not know their grade of listing, but of those that did, ...

- 29% were Grade I
- 55% were Grade II
- 15% were Grade II*
- 1% were Grade III.

The very large majority of listed buildings are Church of England, as Table 63 makes clear. The spread over churchmanships and regions is much more homogeneous than by denomination.

Table 63: Percentage of Listed Buildings (L)
by denomination, churchmanship and region, 1998

Denomination	L%	Churchmanship	L%	Region	L%
Anglican	62	Anglo-Catholic	64	North	26
Baptist	18	Broad	53	Yorks/Humberside	33
Catholic	8	Catholic	24	North West	22
Independent	12	Evan: Broad	37	East Midlands	35
Methodist	10	Evan: Mainstream	21	West Midlands	34
New Church	5	Evan: Charismatic	19	East Anglia	43
Orthodox	26	Evangelical:Total	24	S E (North)	34
Pentecostal	12	Liberal	42	Gr London	25
URC	24	Low Church	34	S E (South)	28
Others	16	Others	10	South West	44

In fact the Church of England, with just over 10,000 listed churches, has four times as many as all the other denominations put together (2,500). The denomination with the next largest number is the Methodists with 600+, trifling by comparison. In 17 counties the

percentage of Anglican churches which are listed is over 80%![21] This
heritage is crippling in terms of the financial burden of upkeep, and
inevitably means that money meant for mission is more difficult to
raise with the momentum of mandatory maintenance.

While all parts of the country have reasonable percentages of listed buildings, the South West and East Anglia have most proportionately and the North West, Greater London and the North the least.

Public toilets

The question was also asked whether the church building, not the
hall, had a public toilet available to the congregation. 60% answered
YES. Again this varied most by denomination more than by churchmanship or region, as Table 64 indicates:

Table 64: Percentage of publicly available toilets (T)
by denomination, churchmanship and region, 1998

Denomination	T %	Churchmanship	T %	Region	T %
Anglican	50	Anglo-Catholic	57	North	57
Baptist	85	Broad	48	Yorks/Humberside	65
Catholic	29	Catholic	45	North West	63
Independent	86	Evan: Broad	69	East Midlands	60
Methodist	74	Evan: Mainstream	85	West Midlands	66
New Church	49	Evan: Charismatic	73	East Anglia	55
Orthodox	72	Evangelical:Total	77	S E (North)	60
Pentecostal	81	Liberal	69	Gr London	68
URC	80	Low Church	63	S E (South)	62
Others	90	Others	22	South West	56

The Roman Catholics and the Anglicans have the smallest percentage of churches with public toilets, along with the New
Churches. Were it not for these the percentage of churches with toilets available would be 80%.

Wheelchair access

Does the church building, not the hall, have wheelchair access? 61%
did, a percentage which like the others, varied most by denomination. Table 65 gives details.

Table 65: Percentage of churches with wheelchair access (W)
by denomination, churchmanship and region, 1998

Denomination	W %	Churchmanship	W %	Region	W %
Anglican	68	Anglo-Catholic	68	North	49
Baptist	68	Broad	61	Yorks/Humberside	64
Catholic	28	Catholic	49	North West	56
Independent	67	Evan: Broad	68	East Midlands	60
Methodist	60	Evan: Mainstream	70	West Midlands	63
New Church	38	Evan: Charismatic	62	East Anglia	62
Orthodox	44	Evangelical:Total	67	S E (North)	62
Pentecostal	59	Liberal	71	Gr London	25
URC	72	Low Church	61	S E (South)	28
Others	68	Others	18	South West	44

The Roman Catholics, New Churches and Orthodox are the only
denominations where under half their churches are not fitted for
wheelchair access. Churches in the North are also just in the same
position.

SUMMARY

1 7,000 churches built before 1300 are still in use at the start of 21st century!

2 One-third of churches in England in 1998 were built in the 20th century, one-third in the 19th, and one-third earlier. 60% of current churches date from 1850.

3 Church closures have been about 6 a week for the last two decades of the 20th century.

4 Church openings were 6 a week from 1980 to 1994, but have been 4 a week since.

5 Most growth in new churches has been in Greater London, the South East and North West.

6 Most new churches are either Pentecostal or New Church, and therefore most new churches are Evangelical.

7 Churches continue to be started in the rural areas to reflect new opportunities even though there are many there already.

8 33% of churches are listed buildings, but 5 in 8, 10,000, are Anglican churches. The burden of upkeep for such must be enormous.

9 60% of churches have a public toilet; 61% wheelchair access.

10 Church growth is still essential; the number of LEPs increases slowly.

NOTES

1. See Brierley, Peter, *'Christian' England*, Page 177f., detailed figures in *Prospects for the Nineties*, 1991, MARC Europe, London, and *Religious Trends* No 2 2000/2001, 1999, HarperCollins and Christian Research, London, Pages 2.3 and 2.4.

2. *Religious Worship in England and Wales*, Census of Great Britain, 1851, George Routledge and Co., London, 1854, Page 102.

3. *The Myth of the Empty Church*, Professor Robin Gill, SPCK, London, 1993.

4. See for example Appendix 3 "Statistics" in *Breaking New Ground, Church Planting in the Church of England*, 1994, Church House Publishing, London, Report commissioned by the House of Bishops, GS 1099, Page 50.

5. Lings, Rev George, *Has Church its Cell Buy Date?*, Encounters on the Edge No 3, July 1999, The Sheffield Centre, Church Army, Page 5.

6. Article *"Current Church Trends in the UK"* part of the "Introduction" in the UK Christian Handbook 1996/97 edition, Christian Research, London, 1995, Page 24, and expanded slightly in Leaders' Briefing No 3 Changing Churches, Brierley, Dr Peter, 1996, Christian Research, London.

7. See article in *Quadrant*, September 1999, Christian Research, London, Page 1.

8. Article by Rev Bob Hopkins and Jon Fox of Anglican Church Planting Initiatives in the *Church of England Newspaper*, 30th April 1999, Page 5.

9. Email from Dr Greg Smith, Research Officer, CREDO, 14th January 1999.

10. The percentages are based on the number of churches in each region in 1998.

11. Article in *Action*, Mission for Christ, Spring 1999, Page 3.

12. *1997 Survey of Rural Services*, 1998, The Rural Development Commission, now part of the Countryside Agency, London, Chapter 8 "Places of worship", Page 110.

13. Ibid, Page 116.

14. Article in *Baptist Times*, 10th June 1999, Page 3.

15. Report to the British Church Growth Association Council Meeting of 9th February 1999 by Rev Dr David Spriggs of the Bible Society.

16. Ibid.

17. Schwarz, Christian, *Natural Church Development, A practical guide to a new approach (in English)*, 1996, British Church Growth Association, Bedford.

18. There is a regular page on Natural Church Development in their magazine *Church Growth Digest*. See, for example, their Volume 20 Number 2 issue, Winter 1998, Page 19.

19. Murray, Rev Dr Stuart, *Church Planting*, 1998, Paternoster Publishing, Carlisle.

20. Op cit (Item 1: Prospects for the Nineties), Page 17.

21. *Religious Trends* No 1, 1998/1999, 1997, Paternoster Publishing, Carlisle, and Christian Research, London, Figure 2.9.5.

9: Still here in 2010?

"We would like to know whether churches will still be here in 10 years time," said one sponsor. But you can hardly ask a church leader, "Will your church survive the next 10 years?" as almost everyone will answer YES. So instead we gave a range of options: "By the year 2010 do you expect your church to have (a) grown significantly, (b) grown a little, (c) remained static, (d) declined, or (e) closed?" The question was not asked in previous surveys.

Still here in 12 years time?

Three-quarters, 77%, of respondents answered this question, which means that we have the replies of over 9,600 churches in England. They answered as follows:

- 33% said they would have grown significantly
- 41% said they would have grown a little
- 12% said they would have remained static
- 8% said they would have declined
- 6% said they would have closed.

If these percentages are applied on a national scale, then three-quarters, 74%, of English churches, nearly 28,000 in total expect to grow over the 12 years 1998-2010. 4,500 will remain static, and 3,000 will have declined. 2,300 will have closed.

As Table 62 showed that 2,767 had actually closed in the last 9 years (which equates to 3,700 closing over 12 years), this last figure of expectations suggests either that some respondents were unduly optimistic (they would not close after all) or didn't wish to face likely reality (perhaps more of those who would have replied "closed" didn't answer the question).

On the other hand it could be argued that their positive approach was very commendable. If decline and closure is expected such outcomes are very likely to happen. "If you set no goals for growth", wrote Robert Schuller, builder of the Crystal Cathedral in California, "you set goals for no growth."[1] "Where there is no visitor, the people perish", said Solomon.[2]

Suppose these predictions became true, and suppose that "significant growth" meant an increase of 20% in Sunday church attendance, "little growth" an increase of 5%, and "declined" meant a drop of 10%. What would Sunday attendance be in 2010 then? It would have increased by just over 40%!

Facing the future by denomination

How do these figures vary by denomination? Table 66 shows us:

Table 66: Expectations for the church growth in 2010, by denomination, 1998

Denomination	Significant growth %	Grown little %	Remained static %	Declined %	Closed %	Total (=100%)
Anglican	29	47	13	7	4	16,281
Baptist	50	38	5	4	3	2,413
R Catholic	11	50	23	14	2	3,771
Independent	45	38	8	5	4	2,243
Methodist	14	40	15	15	16	6,240
New	89	7	0	1	3	1,673
Orthodox	49	32	13	3	3	258
Pentecostal	87	11	1	0	1	2,105
URC	22	50	11	11	6	1,564
Others	30	47	13	6	4	1,169
OVERALL	**33**	**41**	**12**	**8**	**6**	**37,717**

This Table shows that the two denominations most expecting to grow significantly are the New Churches and the Pentecostals. Their expectations are roughly double those of the Baptists, Orthodox and Independents. All of these have seen growth in the past 20 years, though not necessarily since 1989, so their expectation for the future is built in part on their past experience.

The smaller denominations are more cautious, but still a third are anticipating significant growth. These denominations grew significantly in the past. Even if a denomination may decline overall (like the Anglicans and United Reformed) there are always churches within these denominations which grow. Although the growth of individual churches was not measured in the ECAS survey, it was in the 1989 English Church Census. In the 4 years 1985–1989, 18% of the congregations of the smaller denominations grew at least 20%. So did 28% of the Anglicans and 21% of the URC churches. This again suggests, as least for the Anglicans and URC, that the churches expecting growth are looking back at their experience as well as forwards – some have experienced past growth and anticipate the same in the future.

The two denominations where only a small fraction of churches are expecting significant growth are the Roman Catholics and the Methodists. These also were the two which actually grew least 1985-89 (both 16% then). It is these two denominations which have the highest percentages of congregations expecting to be static, again mirroring their experience between 1985 and 1989, although the smaller denominations also had many which were static then.

Between one in 7 and one in 9 Roman Catholic, Methodist or URC churches are expecting to decline in the 12 years 1998 to 2010. One sixth of Methodist congregations expect to close in this period also. Almost half the Methodist churches, 46%, expect to remain either static, decline or close, a situation where morale may well be difficult to change to prevent this becoming reality.

"Some of my attendance figures are this big!"

Facing the future by churchmanship

How do these figures vary by churchmanship? As might otherwise be expected, in many ways the next Table to some extent reflects the churchmanship make up of the different denominations, as can be seen:

Table 67: Expectations for the church growth in 2010, by churchmanship, 1998

Churchmanship	Significant growth %	Grown little %	Remained static %	Declined %	Closed %	Total (=100%)
Anglo-Catholic	24	55	13	7	1	**2,012**
Broad	14	49	19	11	7	**4,996**
Catholic	15	52	21	11	1	**5,824**
Evangelical: Broad	25	51	14	7	3	**3,505**
Evangelical: Main.	43	42	6	5	4	**6,105**
Evangelical: Charis	79	18	1	1	1	**4,790**
Evangelical: Total	51	36	6	4	3	**14,400**
Liberal	17	51	15	11	6	**4,622**
Low Church	18	42	16	15	9	**4,501**
Others	16	32	11	5	36	**1,362**
OVERALL	**33**	**41**	**12**	**8**	**6**	**37,717**

This Table shows the tremendous confidence in Charismatic churches for strong growth in the decade ahead. Four out of 5 Charismatic churches are predicting significant growth, a percentage almost twice as high as that which the mainstream Evangelicals are anticipating. Outside these two, the other churchmanships are much more modest, collectively 18%.

These differences continue across the rest of the Table. Apart from the Mainstream and Charismatic Evangelicals, half, 49%, of the rest of the churchmanships together are expecting some growth, with one in six, 17%, expecting to remain static.

The greatest difference however is with the small number of other churchmanships, those who described themselves in unconventional ways. Over a third of these reckon they will be closed within the next 12 years. This may reflect the lack of support found in belonging to a large established group and inadequate economic viability.

These variations are illustrated in Figure 45, and show the huge expectations of the Charismatics.

Figure 45: Expectations of congregations 1998-2010 by churchmanship

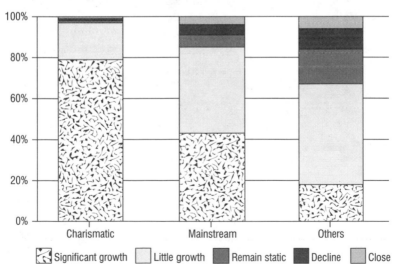

*Figure 46a: Expectations of congregations to grow significantly by 2010
by region*

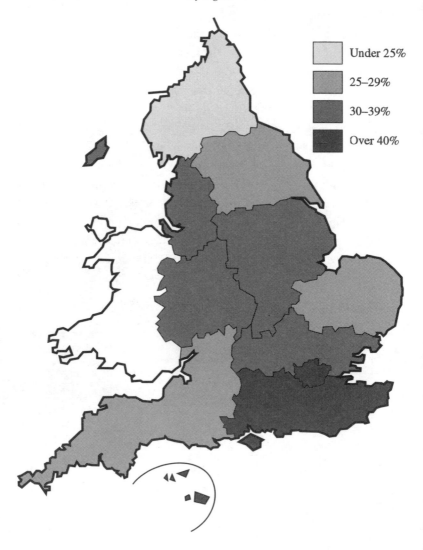

Figure 46b: Expectations of congregations to decline or close by 2010
by region

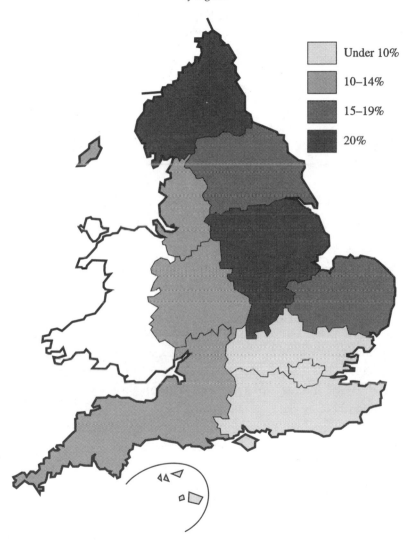

Facing the future by region

The next Table shows how these figures vary by different parts of the country:

Table 68: Expectations for the church in 2010, by region, 1998

Region	Significant growth %	Grown little %	Remained static %	Declined %	Closed %	Total (=100%)
North	23	42	15	13	7	2,443
Yorks/Humberside	28	42	14	8	8	3,606
North West	31	44	11	10	4	4,044
East Mids	30	36	14	11	9	3,856
West Mids	31	44	12	8	5	3,790
East Anglia	27	43	12	9	9	2,662
S E (North)	36	43	12	6	3	3,800
Greater London	49	37	7	4	3	3,743
S E (South)	41	41	9	5	4	4,212
South West	29	42	15	7	7	5,561
OVERALL	**33**	**41**	**12**	**8**	**6**	37,717

As with other questions in the English Church Attendance Survey, regional variations are much more muted, and this is true of growth expectations. Half the churches in Greater London expect to grow significantly, and two-fifths of those in South East South, and fewer churches here expect to remain static.

One church in five, 20%, in the North and East Midlands expect to decline or close by 2010, a percentage almost half as big again as elsewhere in the country, except East Anglia where 18% of congregations say the same. As Figure 46 on the previous pages shows, it is the eastern part of the country where expectations to decline or close are strongest, other than the South East. This tallies with where the growth that has happened has taken place.

Facing the future by age-group

The next Table shows how each type of growth/decline/closure vary by the age-groups in each congregation. Note that the percentages adding to 100% go downwards not across in this Table.

Table 69: Age-group percentages for differing expectations by 2010, 1998

Age-group	Significant growth %	Grown little %	Remained static %	Declined %	Closed %	Overall
Under 15	20	18	22	17	9	19
15 to 19	7	6	5	4	3	6
20 to 29	12	9	8	6	4	9
30 to 44	22	17	14	14	7	17
45 to 64	22	25	24	23	22	24
65 and over	17	24	27	35	55	25
TOTAL (=100%)	12,447	15,464	4,526	3,017	2,263	37,717

This Table shows that it is the churches with the greatest proportion of older people who expect either to close or decline. Those who expect to grow significantly are those with an above average number in their 20s and aged 30 to 44, that is, of people of whom many will be parents with young children. That is, they have people with energy, probable commitment and maybe willingness to learn leadership. Perhaps this is one of the chief priorities that the Charismatic churches can teach others – learn to relate to parents, and win them. Churches expecting to grow only a little do not have an above average percentage of children or teenagers, though those declining or closing are below average.

Facing the future by frequency of attendance

The next Table shows the proportions by frequency of Sunday attendance by the various changes that may take place by 2010. Again the percentages add downwards.

Table 70: Frequency of attendance percentages
for differing expectations by 2010, 1998

Frequency	Significant growth %	Grown little %	Remained static %	Declined %	Closed %	Overall
Twice a week	18	10	7	9	7	12
Weekly	44	46	47	51	42	46
Fortnightly	11	11	9	10	15	11
Monthly	8	9	9	8	15	9
Quarterly	4	5	6	5	6	5
Twice a year	15	19	22	17	15	17
TOTAL (=100%)	12,447	15,464	4,526	3,017	2,263	37,717

Table 70 indicates that the churches where attendance twice a week is greatest are likely to be those expecting significant growth. Those remaining static have many who come just twice a year, and those who expect to closer have above average proportions attending just fortnightly or monthly, maybe because their churches are already holding services only every two or four weeks.

Facing the future by size of church

The final Table shows the proportions by size of existing congregation for the various changes that may take place by 2010.

Table 71: Expectations for 2010 by size of congregation, 1998

Congregation size	Significant growth %	Grown little %	Remained static %	Declined %	Closed %	Overall
25 or less	14	40	21	15	10	8,047
26 to 50	29	49	12	9	1	7,198
51 to 100	41	45	9	5	0	9,000
101 to 150	48	42	6	4	0	4,345
151 to 200	53	37	7	3	0	2,524
201 to 300	49	39	8	4	0	2,518
Over 300	38	40	14	8	0	4,085
OVERALL	33	41	12	8	6	37,717

This Table shows that over half, 54%, of the smallest churches are expecting growth in the period up to 2010. Three-quarters, 78%, of churches with congregations between 26 and 50 are expecting the same, with nearly a third, 29%, expecting significant growth. Whilst it is good to admire this optimism, it must be said that these outcomes are highly unlikely humanly speaking. In the decade 1979 to 1989 half of the churches with congregations under 50 closed. Are these results because respondents do not wish to face up to the future the see, and hope against hope, for something else? Or are they just being totally unrealistic as to what is possible? Either way, we have a serious problem with false expectations.

The Table also shows that the percentage expecting significant growth increases as the size of the congregation increases up to 200. Thereafter it decreases, and one church in 7, 14%, of the largest churches expect to remain static. Indeed one church in 8, 12%, in this group expect to decline by 2010.

The optimum church size, judging by the largest percentages expecting to grow are with congregation between 100 and 150 or 151 and 200. It was churches of these sizes in 1989 which had experienced the greatest rates of growth over the previous 4 years. Churches of these sizes invariably are "one-man bands", that is, looked after by one full-time salaried minister. To grow larger than 200 requires a second full-time person to help, either an assistant pastor/curate, or church secretary/administrator. For most people there is a limit of 200 faces that they can recognise and name, which can be proven mathematically (it comes then to 168). The second person needs to be appointed before growth can be expected. Of course two people working together form a different kind of team from that which operated before, and not every minister can handle this transition.

So where does all this take us?

The churches which are expecting to grow significantly by 2010 are especially the Charismatic churches, followed by the Mainstream Evangelical churches. Many of the subsequent characteristics simply follow the characteristics of these churches, such as age and frequency of attendance. They also reflect the denominational composition, where New and Pentecostal Churches are by far the most numerous in those expecting significant growth.

The dominant factor is churchmanship more than denomination, and the vision and expectation that is built in with that. Do other churches wish to share in that vision? What needs to be done to help it to be shared?

There are also many churches whose anticipation of the future is almost certainly unrealistic, "over the top" as some would say. It is critical that such leaders are helped before their congregation withers through disillusionment. Can this be a major reason why people change church they can see the church is not getting anyway despite grand gestures for gaining growth?

However it does seem that the experience that individual churches have had of growth in the past, as mirrored in denominational percentages, may well significantly determine their expectations for the future. This is understandable, as success breeds success. But how can the mould be broken, so that churches and denominations which do not have a record of growth begin to believe that change is possible? This is the subject of the final chapter.

SUMMARY

1 At least 7 in every 8 New and Pentecostal Churches expect to see significant growth in the 12 years 1998 to 2010.

2 One Methodist church in 6 expects to close by 2010.

3 The clearest distinguishing characteristic determining whether a church expects to grow significantly by 2010 is their churchmanship.

4 Four Charismatic churches in 5, 79%, expect to grow significantly in the 12 years 1998 to 2010, and 3 in every 7 mainstream Evangelical churches, 43%. Only a sixth, 18%, of churches with other churchmanships expect to do so.

5 There are relatively few regional differences, although half the churches in Greater London expect to grow significantly by 2010, and one fifth in the North or East Midlands expect to decline or close.

6 Churches expecting to grow significantly have a third, 34%, of their congregation aged between 20 and 44, the age of many younger parents.

7 Churches expecting to close have over half their congregation over 65 years of age.

8 Churches expecting to grow significantly have more people coming twice a week. Churches who expect to remain static have a higher percentage of people coming just twice a year. Churches expecting to close have more people coming just fortnightly or monthly.

9 If a congregation is under 100 people it may well mean that the pastor is unrealistically expecting growth, or too much growth too soon. A few of the largest congregations are anticipating decline.

10 How may the expectancy and experience of Charismatic and Mainstream Evangelical churches best be shared? Do other churches want to have it or are fatalism and apathy 'giants' too big to be overcome?

NOTES

1. Schuller, Rev Robert, *Your Church has a Fantastic Future,* 1986, Regal Books, Ventura, California.
2. Proverbs chapter 18 verse 29.

10: All over bar the shouting?

The English Church Attendance Survey has revealed some unpalatable things about the church for the start of the 21st century. Is this the end of the church? Is it all over bar the shouting? NO! And a thousand times NO!

Why not? Jesus was very clear: "I will build my church," He said[1], and whilst that doesn't presume there will be no closures or downsizing, overall He is in the business of finding a people to share eternity with Him. Despite the huge mass of parachurch organisations all trying to help it forward, 5,600 in 2000[2], Jesus did not say, "I will build my parachurch." So what is church?

The ECAS study defined a church as a body of people meeting on a Sunday in the same premises primarily for public worship at regular intervals. This definition relates to people meeting, interacting, forming friendships, enjoying fellowship and interacting in other ways. Church is people, not a building. Secondly they come together for worship, often especially around the Eucharist, Lord's Supper, Holy Communion, Mass, etc. They do so in the context of Christian instruction, implicit or explicit, often in the form of a sermon. They do so at regular intervals. This conforms to what those did who formed the very first church "they met constantly to hear the apostles, teach, and to share the common life, to break bread and to pray."[3]

Survey summary

What the survey has shown is:

- Sunday church attendance in England has dropped a million people in the 9 years 1989 to 1998, and was 7.5% of the population in 1998
- A third of that drop is due to people attending less frequently, on average fortnightly rather than weekly; 10.2% of the population attend once a month
- Half of the decline is amongst children under 15 years of age
- One person in 8 going to church is non-white
- Evangelicals have declined less than non-evangelicals; the Mainstream have grown while Broad and Charismatic Evangelicals have decreased
- Two churches in 5 hold a midweek worship service, attended by 0.5% of the population. One in 7 holds a special Youth service, attended by 0.4% of the population over a month.
- In the late 1990s there were far fewer new churches being started than in the early 1990s
- It is the Charismatics who have the greatest expectancy of significant growth by 2010, but they account for only 14% of all English churchgoers.

Giving it perspective

This can rightly be seen as a crisis situation, but even so it needs to be put into perspective. Large scale measurements of church attendance are few. The first count of attendance was in 1851 as part of the Census of Population of England and Wales. Depending on how the figures are taken, the percentage attending church on Census Sunday was 39% but this included those who went two or three times[4]. If the same percentage of "twicers" which was counted in 1903 applied in 1851 (and it could have been more then), then this figure would reduce to 24%.

A major large scale study of London[5] was undertaken by the *Daily News* between November 1902 and November 1903. This sought to count everyone entering every place of worship in a specific Borough of London for every service, counting a different Borough each week. The conclusion of the report's author is interesting: "The outstanding lesson of the Census is that the power of preaching is undiminished. Wherever there is the right man in the pulpit there are few, if any, empty pews."[6] *Excluding* twicers, the percentage of the population who attended church in London was 19% each Sunday.

A survey by the research organisation Mass-Observation in 1948/49 found that 15% of the population attended church[7]. The English Church Census found it was 12% in 1979 and 10% in 1989. This survey puts it at 7.5%. It is obvious from Figure 47 that the gentle slope of decline over the last 150 years has started to accelerate.

Figure 47: Church attendance in England 1851-1998

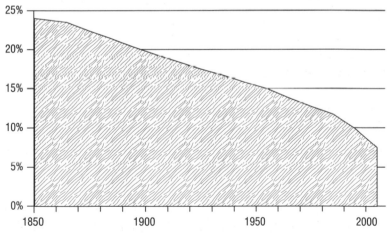

It is equally clear that the context of what it means to go to church has changed. On a monthly basis the percentage of the population attending church sometime during the month is 11.1%[8], as illustrated in Figure 48, more than in 1989, but then some of the components of the 11.1% were not measured in 1989.

Figure 48 is a simple pie chart which reflects an important change that is already in process. Church culture is changing; what we used to mean by "church" is becoming something of the past. People are voting with their feet and doing new things, and far thinking church leaders in many cases are encouraging it.

Figure 48: Church attendance over a month, 1998

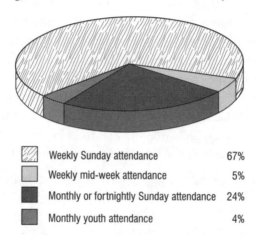

	Weekly Sunday attendance	67%
	Weekly mid-week attendance	5%
	Monthly or fortnightly Sunday attendance	24%
	Monthly youth attendance	4%

Counting church people

This implies a suggestion or recommendation for churches: In future perhaps what should be counted are **the number of people (including children and young people) attending worship services either on Sunday or mid-week, averaged over a month.**

There are a number of criteria relevant to collecting church statistics.

- Firstly, they need to be *nationally* collected, that is, every Diocese, Association, District, Province, etc. should collect them on the same basis.

- Secondly they need to be *comparable* to other denominations and to previous figures. This latter point means that the numbers attending weekly on a Sunday need to be separately maintained, so that it can be seen what proportion they are of the total (67% in Figure 48), and also to ensure continuity with figures previously collected. Historical sequences are important.

- Thirdly they must be *useful to respondents,* so it is essential that they are fed back to them, ideally with trends and a picture over a larger area.

- Fourthly they should be *easy to collect,* because good response is important for accuracy, and when clergy are under pressure, it is necessary to minimise the time and trouble involved in providing them.

It might be argued that focussing on monthly attendance rather than weekly might encourage those who attend fortnightly only to come once a month. That may be true, but it might also cause those who come once a quarter to come once a month instead.

It would help if churches instead of providing weekly news sheets provided monthly ones instead. Then if a regular churchgoer missed week 2 for example they could still find out what was happening that month.

Children

But we must not let ourselves be fooled. The situation is much more serious than just playing around with statistics. The churches must not ape what Margaret Thatcher did with the unemployment figures to find a more palatable measure which will go down better with the media. That simply will not do. Wrote Graham Mytton, former Head of Research of BBC World Service, "Research is as important as ever but its priority becomes to understand audiences better, not merely to be able to count them."[9]

We cannot ignore the fact that 2,200 people are ceasing attending church on a Sunday *every week*. 1,000 of these are boys and girls aged under 15. This is a horrific figure. We are losing more children in the 1990s than we lost children, youth and adults together in the 1980s. We simply have **got** to focus, or re-focus on children's work.

That will inevitably mean doing *more work with schools*. Many schools already have clergy and lay Christian people as governors, and allow access to children for Assemblies or RE lessons. Christian teachers need to be supported and prayed for specifically. Some parachurch organisations like Youth for Christ have huge opportunities, mostly in school Assemblies. Two-thirds, 65%, of the 48,000 children they contacted in 1997 were under 15 years of age[10].

In the process of working with children, we cannot avoid moving in some of the areas where they move. One of the more crucial is *technology*. Most are totally at home with computers, and many with the Internet. One of the dangers is the access that gives to paedophiles and pornography[11]. One of the consequences is the strengthening of mosaic thinking.

Some organisations have found one major opportunity with young people is encouraging them to pray, and engaging them to be pray-ers.

Young People

Just because some of the teenagers are switching into midweek special youth services, we must not assume that we have solved the problem of reaching the teens and the twenties. "A major cause of decline is the sheer mediocrity and dullness of the religious life of the mainstream. Frankly it is boring. It opens no windows in the soul. ... As Nietzsche once observed, its members do not *look* redeemed."[12]

Teenagers are invited to explore a wide variety of other beliefs. One book which was sent unasked to the Christian Research office was called *How to turn your ex-boyfriend into a toad and other spells*, with the subtitle *"for love, wealth, beauty and revenge"*. It contained real spells but had a note as a legal safeguard "the spells in this book are for entertainment only"[13]. It was aimed at teenage girls as far as we could tell.

With the UK and other Western governments shifting more of the cost of public education on to the middle class, it is likely that older teens and those in their 20s who go on the further education will graduate with serious debt burdens[14]. For Christians, that impinges on their ability to give to the church, or to save so they can take an additional course at a Bible College, for example. It is thought that as they grow older they "will not even be able to sustain the present giving levels to the church and its mission let alone increase them."[15] If this proves true, that is likely to have serious repercussions on churches and the many parachurch agencies which rely on voluntary contributions. Giving levels to the Anglican church in 1997 were an estimated 3.2% of take-home pay[16].

We need to *involve young people in leadership,* and learn from them initiatives, ideas and creativity. One parachurch organisation I know appointed a young man in his mid-20s to its Board last year. A large Anglican church in south London, with 400+ attending, approved a 27 year old as one of its two churchwardens in April 1999. The Church of England formed the Archbishop's Council at the beginning of 1999 as it restructured following the Turnbull Report[17] of the Bishop of Durham; it deliberately contained several younger people.

It is crucial to focus on the needs of this age-group. For example, one societal trend in this age-group is the increasing number of single mums. When American futurologist Tom Sine asked their needs at a seminar, the reply was: "Child care, emotional and economic support systems."[18] How would young people in your church create programmes to meet these needs? One central London church discovered an above average number of single mums in its neighbourhood, and specially proceeded to train those willing to call and befriend them. The principle here is *building real friendship, not just charitable concern or specious fellowship.*

Some in this age-group will be *radical*. "Radical is not multi-coloured hair. Radical is not cool clothes and designer shoes. ... Radical is knowing how to – and being willing to – get to the root of it all. It's the ability to cut to the core of what is right and wrong with the world."[19] In the Meredith Belbin leadership test creativity and problem-solving, being radical, come together. "A radical life is knowing God so well you can pray once and the heavens close for three years and then pray again and see fire fall from the sky, yet still be a man of passions like any one of us (see 1 Kings 17, 18). Posers are plenty. We are badly in need of some real radicals."[20] A number of Christian leaders now in their 40s and early 50s were radicals 20 years ago. How do we find the space for radicals today?

A number of these young leaders would be enormously enriched by suitable, understanding, *mentors*. Can we find those willing to stand alongside them, listen to them, understand them, and give them permission to make mistakes? Mentoring could mean reading the same passages of Scriptures over a period of say 2 weeks and then noting the issues which inspired them, going to church together and discussing impressions of the service, working together in some form of community service, debating such questions as "Why I like being a Methodist (or Baptist or whatever)", and if possible attending a church Diaconate or Council meeting and discussing its process[21].

One church *paired up* its young people with an older member of the congregation. The older and younger person were encouraged to get to know each other and pray for each other. One month a year they were expected to attend together everything that each normally went to. It's led to some deep friendships across generations, and a fresh understanding of the opportunities and pressures each face.

Pastor Richard James was asked to lead St David's Anglican church in Forestville, a Sydney suburb in Australia. The church was hidden behind beautiful gum trees, and everyone passing on the nearby highway missed it. So he copied McDonald's and introduced a drive-thru church! Several times a year, volunteers from the church lined a mile stretch of road during the morning rush hour, beckoning commuters to pull in for a moment. They gave each a tape of sermons, and at Christmas a coke and cake. The community now knows the church is there; many drop in.[22] A radical idea that worked!

Consider the parents

Parents, those aged 30 to 44, are beginning to leave the church. They didn't in the 1980s, but have started to do so in the 1990s, because they are "too busy". But that simply means they have other priorities. Why?

We need to encourage more *personal spirituality*. In congregational studies we have undertaken, there has been a close association between feeling close to God in worship and growth in faith. Mother Theresa once wrote, "Try to put worship into practice in your life. Be alone with Jesus. You will notice a change in your life, in your family, in your parish and in your environment."[23] 35% of churchgoers spend at least an hour in personal prayer each week[24]. Can we encourage more prayer, by introducing Prayer triplets or Prayer Diaries?

Some in this age-group need *more help to understand the Scriptures*. The younger a person, the less the private reading of the Bible[25]. Can we encourage more reading of the Scriptures perhaps by helping those new to the faith to find their way round it? Or encourage all the congregation to read the same passage every day. Or promote Bible reading schemes. One of the main differences between North American church life and British is the widespread acceptance in North America of what they call "Adult Sunday Schools". These are really like Home Study groups, but because they invariably meet on Sunday mornings before church, they encourage greater church attendance. However I believe one of their key functions is to allow people to ask simple questions about the Bible without embarrassment. UK Alpha groups allow the same which is one reason for their popularity with existing churchgoers.

There is another factor also. People need to *belong before they believe*. Canon Geoffrey Walker, Bath & Wells Diocesan Missioner, is certain of this and describes the accompanying process of conversion as "a process of socialisation, biographical reconstruction which goes hand-in-hand with the discipling process"[26]. What he means is that young, middle class urban professionals in cities like London join a church group which helps them turn from the old life into the new life the church offers in Christ. In this way the cultural adaptation begins, the process of the "survival of a colony within an alien society"[27]. An Australian survey found that "almost all newcomers spoke about the importance of the friendliness of the church that was offered without any strings attached"[28]. This was especially true, "a vital sign of friendliness"[29], if it did not matter if their children made a noise in the service.

Many people of this age-group are working, and for those who are Christian, witness by deed as well as word is part of their way of life. They do not often however get much encouragement in their church for *expressing their Christian standards at work*. One study showed that in some matters (like saying the boss was out when s/he was in) there was no difference between Christian and non-Christian[30]. When Chief Executive Officers of Christian organisations meeting in September 1999 were asked a key way to turn the church round, they replied, "We must make our Christianity work in the office and the pub more than church."[31] They also suggested having a "Businessman's Alpha" in the workplace. People at work "need to earn the right to be heard by the intrinsic sense of what they say, and by their own integrity and credibility"[32].

There are also many Christians in this age-group or the next who are *aware of failure*. They proclaim their own faith, but somehow their own children have not followed them in it. The same is true of many clergy families. Some in this age-group have failed themselves, and have seen their family split apart in divorce. This is not new, but the pain is still very real. J H F Piele wrote a book called *"Reproach of the Gospel: Inquiry into apparent failure of Christianity as a general rule of life and conduct with special reference to the present time"* – it was published in 1909![33] Such happenings can greatly inhibit witness, or can sometimes be used to exhibit the gospel's power to triumph in adverse circumstances.

The grandparents

The oldies are coming back! One of the surprising statistics which emerged when compiling *Religious Trends* No 2 was the realisation that before the First World War *more than half* the children went to Sunday School every week! A similar high percentage continued up to the 1930s. These children are now grandparents, and perhaps part of their journey back is their childhood memories. It is also another reason why half the audience of *Songs of Praise* is over 65.

A number of people of this broad age-group, 45 and over, are teaching in Sunday School (younger people not being available or willing). Some are taking initiatives to help other oldies, like holding luncheon clubs once a week or fortnight, or coffee mornings. Some have initiated Oldies Bible Study groups. How can we help these people, often with energy, health, and because of earlier retirement, free time, to *use their gifts constructively* to reach out?

Inevitably older people eventually get "promoted to glory", as the Salvation Army puts it. We need to encourage and enable them into mission while we still have them!

Thinking strategically

"What is the most important characteristic to measure in churchgoers?" was the question Keith Danby, Chief Executive of book wholesalers STL, asked in a Bolton seminar in May 1998. The answer given was "Age". Consequently the above comments have been broken down by rough age-group to illustrate key areas for possible future action.

The basic purpose of this book is to report the outcome of the English Church Attendance Survey. But as the findings are so stark it would be wrong not to stand on the foundation of these statistics and peer into the future. We are losing people very fast, and like the water which poured into the *Titanic* and caused its buoyancy to go, we cannot continue to lose so many without our buoyancy also going.

This is not a futuristic book like Tom Sine's *Mustard Seed versus McWorld* or Kenneth Leech's *The Sky is Red*[34]. These two books gaze into the Christian future in the UK and the West with some uncomfortable conclusions. The first, written from an evangelical perspective, suggests many excellent models to take the church forward into a changed but sustainable framework with a deep sense of the call to touch society. The second, a brilliant exposition by an Anglo-Catholic, challenges us likewise to be committed to people, seeing the survival of Christianity as mainly in the more fundamentalist camp (something which the results of ECAS bear out).

I am a statistician, not a theologian. The numbers in this book show a haemorrhage akin to a burst artery. The country is littered with people who used to go to church but no longer do. We could well bleed to death. The tide is running out. At the present rate of change we are one generation from extinction. But it is not yet all over bar the shouting. Strategic thinking can be done. Action is possible. Thinking future is not just something that the five wise virgins did in Jesus' parable, when they asked the unspoken questions: What if he takes longer than anyone thinks? What if he, for his own reasons, delays his coming? What must we do to get ready for such a possibility? What can we do while we wait for him?[35]

As a church we are weak in thinking strategically. We have not planned for, nor managed, strategic change in the societal impact on our church life. The Anglicans, Baptists, Methodists and even the New Churches have all changed or re-evaluated their central structures in the 1990s. That process needs continuing in other areas of church life. One comment made by *The Tablet* when Maryvale Pastoral Centre closed was that it reflected "the lack of a church strategy at national level"[36].

A J Toynbee, the historian, says in his book *An Historian's Approach to Religion*, that when a movement faces a crisis it can take one of several ways out. First, it can retreat into the past and glory in what it was. Toynbee calls that archaism. Second, it can leap into the future and build castles in the air; it can dream of what it would like to do. That he calls futurism. Third, it can retreat into itself and give itself to mystical experiences. His term for that is mysticism. Fourth, it can take hold of the crisis, transform it into something positive and make a fresh beginning. He calls that re-formation. Only the last solution resolves the problem; the rest are short-lived.[37] I would add a fifth, though. The church can be apathetic and unwilling to change, lacking energy to do so, or lacking the leadership to stir it afresh. That is defeatism. We still need the fourth – re-formation. Pope Paul says, "Europe can choose between nihilism and the rediscovery of the Christian faith"[38]. Let us choose to go on living!

Conclusion

Tony Compolo, the American sociologist and evangelist, tells the story of two young sons, one of whom was a great optimist and the other a born pessimist. To redress the balance, their parents decided one Christmas to fill their sacks with different things.

The pessimist's sack was full of every toy they could think of that would delight him. But the optimist's they filled with manure. On Christmas morning, their pessimistic son wasn't unduly moved by the abundance of gifts. Yet the excited response of their optimistic son was puzzling, until he cried, "Thank you, oh, thank you, I just know there's a pony outside somewhere!"[39]

Where are the visionaries who can see the pony? Where are the Christian leaders and lay people who can see vibrant, overflowing churches and a nation turning back to God? Or Ezekiel's valley of dry bones[40] as an army for the Kingdom?

SUMMARY

1 "Church attendance drops a million in 9 years" is a crisis head-line, especially when half that decline is from children under 15 years of age.

2 It is suggested that in future we count church attendance per month at worship services, Sunday and midweek.

3 Focus urgently on children. Understand their technological world. Work more with schools where contact with most of the nation's children is guaranteed.

4 Continue to focus on teens and twenties, where the church is weakest. Look for the radicals! Bring young people into leadership.

5 Encourage personal spirituality, especially amongst those aged 30 to 44, who are beginning to leave in large numbers.

6 Teach church people the Christian faith, as well as non-church people.

7 Challenge churchgoers to foster fervent friendship with unbelievers.

8 Help Christian people to witness in their world of work.

9 Enable older people to reach out in mission while we still have them.

10 We urgently need to expect and plan to manage strategic change. The existing church culture needs radical overhaul and renewal.

NOTES

1. Matthew chapter 16 verse 18.
2. Wraight, Heather, editor, *UK Christian Handbook,* 2000/2001 edition, 1999, HarperCollinsReligious and Christian Research, London, Table 1.
3. Acts of the Apostles chapter 2 verse 42.
4. Mann, Horace, *Religious Worship in England and Wales,* Census of Great Britain 1851, 1854, George Routledge & Co., London.
5. Mudie-Smith, Richard, *The Religious Life of London,* 1904, Hodder & Stoughton, London.
6. Ibid., Page 7.
7. Report of Mass-Observation survey in 1949, published originally in *British Weekly,* Jan/Feb 1949, and also in Winter, 1952, edition of *Vision,* Volume III, Number 1, Journal of the Free Church of England, Page 1. Original report in the Mass-Observation Archive in the University of Sussex, Brighton.
8. Made up of 10.2% attending on a Sunday and 0.9% mid-week.
9. Article *"Changes in Research Strategy"* in *Catalyst,* Summer 1999, ICMC, Keighley, West Yorkshire, Page 4.
10. *FactFile* Number 5, Summer 1998, Youth For Christ, Birmingham, and Christian Research, London, Page 2.
11. Sine, Dr Tom, *Mustard Seed versus McWorld,* 1999, Monarch Publications, Crowborough, East Sussex, Page 99.
12. Leech, Rev Kenneth, *The Sky is Red,* 1998, Darton, Longman and Todd, London, Page 113.
13. By Gray, Deborah and Starwoman, Athena, 1996, HarperCollins Publishers, London.
14. Op cit (Item 11), Page 135.
15. Op cit (Item 11), Page 194.
16. Report *"Church giving needs to hot up"* in *Church Times,* 28th May 1999.
17. Turnbull, Rt Rev Michael, *One Body,* 1997, Church House Publishing, London.
18. Op cit (Item 11), Page 54.
19. Pratney, Dr Winkie, *Fire on the Horizon,* 1999, Gospel Light, Ventura, California, Page 179.
20. Ibid.
21. Hanerwas and Williamson, *Resident Aliens,* 1989, Abingdon Press, Nashville, United States, Page 106f.
22. Report in *Leadership* magazine, Spring 1999, Page 11.
23. de Bertodano, Teresa, *Daily Readings with Mother Teresa,* 1993, Fount, HarperCollinsPublishers, London, Page 68.

24. Survey by Teal Trust, Cramlington, reported in *Quadrant,* May 1999, Christian research, London, Page 1.
25. Brierley, Dr Peter, *Twelve Things to Wake Up to!,* 1999, Christian Research, London, Page 11.
26. Personal email of 13th January 1999.
27. Op cit (Item 21), Page 115.
28. Hughes, Rev Dr Philip, *Report on Congregational Health and Vitality in the Anglican Diocese of Melbourne,* 1998, Christian Research Association, Victoria, Australia, Page 27.
29. Ibid.
30. Report of the *Ansvar Survey of English Social Behaviour* in special issue of *Quadrant,* November 1995, Christian Research, London.
31. A CEO Forum at High Leigh Conference Centre, organised with the help of the Evangelical Alliance and Global Connections.
32. Op cit (Item 12), Page 108.
33. By Longmans Green, London.
34. Op cit (Items 11 and 12).
35. Op cit (Item 19), Page 149.
36. *The Tablet,* 3rd-10th April, 1999.
37. From Hughes, Selwyn, *Every Day with Jesus,* CWR, Farnham, Surrey, notes for 11th July 1999.
38. Cited in op cit (Item 12) from Peter Hebbelthwaite, *National Catholic Reporter,* 13th December 1991.
39. From an article *"Hope in a hopeless world"* in *Compass,* the quarterly journal of non-religious Christianity, Pioneer, Farnham, Surrey, Autumn 1999, Page 12.
40. Ezekiel chapter 37 verses 1–14.

Appendix

English Church Attendance Survey

Church Details

1. Name of Church/Fellowship (if different from above) _____

2. Postal Address of Church/Venue (if different from above) _____

_____ Postcode_____

3. Church Telephone No (if any) _____ Fax No (if any)_____

E-mail No (if any)_____ 4. In what year was this church/fellowship founded?_____

5. Is the Church building a Listed Building? YES/NO   If YES, please give Grade if known _____

6. Does your Church (not hall) have a toilet publicly available to congregation? YES/NO   Wheelchair access? YES/NO

Church Leadership

7. Title and name of (Senior) Minister/Leader (if different from above): _____

Position: Minister/Vicar/Rector/Priest/Pastor/Leader/Other _____ Address_____

_____ Postcode_____

Tel No_____ Fax No_____ E-mail No_____

8. Title and name of other ordained staff (if any): _____

Position: Minister/Vicar/Rector/Priest/Pastor/Leader/Other _____ Address_____

_____ Postcode_____ Tel No _____

9a. Name of person responsible for children's work with under 12s: Mr/Mrs/Ms/Miss_____

Address_____ Postcode_____ Tel No _____

9b. Name of person responsible for young people's work with 12s and over: Mr/Mrs/Ms/Miss_____

Address_____ Postcode_____ Tel No _____

9c. Do you have a full-time salaried youth worker? YES/NO   If YES, please give name and address: Mr/Mrs/Ms/Miss ____

_____ Address_____

_____ Postcode_____ Tel No _____

10. Please give name, position, address and telephone number of any other ordained/full-time pastoral staff on a separate sheet of paper.

11. Is the person in Q7 responsible for other congregations as well?   YES/NO   If YES how many?_____

A form should have been received for each church for which this person is responsible. If not, please write below the details of other churches or attach a list so that we can check our records.

Name _____   _____   _____

Location _____   _____   _____

Attendance

12. Please estimate the **average number** on a typical Saturday/Sunday in September 1998 at this church. (Please count any adults or children who attend more than one Saturday/Sunday service only once.)

Total number of adults (aged 15 and above) _____ Total number of children (aged 14 and under)_____

Frequency

13. We appreciate that it is difficult, but it would be a great help if you could estimate the approximate numbers of your **total** adult congregation who attend Saturday/Sunday services on a weekly, fortnightly, monthly, and less frequent basis.

Twice weekly_____ Weekly_____ Fortnightly_____ Monthly_____ Quarterly_____ Twice a year _____

Are these figures estimated? ☐   or counted? ☐ (tick one only)   Visitors/first attendance_____

Age

14. Please could you estimate the approximate numbers of your congregation who attend Saturday/Sunday services who fall into the following age groups.

Under 15_____ 15 to 19_____ 20 to 29_____ 30 to 44_____ 45 to 64_____ 65 and over _____

Ethnic

15. Please could you estimate the approximate numbers of your adult congregation who fall into the following ethnic groups.

White_____ Black Caribbean/African/Black Other_____ Chinese/Korean/Japanese _____

Indian/Pakistani/Bangladeshi_____ Other Asian_____ Other Non-white _____

Churchmanship

16. Which of these terms, or which combination of them, would best describe your congregation? **Please tick no more than three**

Anglo-Catholic ☐	Charismatic ☐	Low Church ☐	Other ☐
Broad ☐	Evangelical ☐	Orthodox ☐	Please specify _____
Catholic ☐	Liberal ☐	Radical ☐	

Mid-Week

17. Do you have a regular mid-week worship service? YES/NO If YES, roughly how many come? _____

18. Do you have a regular Youth worship service?   YES/NO If YES, roughly how many come? _____

19. Please could you estimate roughly how many (fringe) people usually attend mid-week church run activities (such as Drop in Centre, Mothers & Toddlers), but do not regularly attend worship services. (Please exclude outside organisations who hire or make use of your church premises)

Number of adults (aged 15 and above)_____ Number of children (aged 14 and under) _____

Other

20. If your Church has any of these ministries please tick appropriately:

Regular Healing services   ☐   Counselling style healing ministry by minister/overall leader ☐
Laying on of hands etc, at other times ☐   Counselling style healing ministry by lay people   ☐

21. By 2010 do you expect your church to have (please tick ONE only)

Grown significantly ☐   Grown a little ☐   Remained static ☐   Declined ☐   Closed ☐

Name of respondent (IN CAPITALS PLEASE)_____

Telephone No _____   Date_____

Thank you very much for your help. Please return the form to English Church Attendance Survey, Vision Building, 4 Footscray Road, Eltham, London SE9 2TZ in the envelope provided. Telephone 0181-294 1989 Fax 0181-294 0014

From time to time we make our mailing list available to other charities and companies offering services relevant to church work today. Should you not wish to be on that mailing list please tick the box.☐

Index

*The letter "f" following a page number means that page
and the two following consecutive pages*